Responsibilities in Action

Understanding the Connections

The Massachusetts
Medication Administration Program
Certification Training

To the Reader

Re·spon·si·bil·i·ty - The state or fact of being accountable or answerable for something.

'Responsibilities in Action' is based on the concept that a set of responsibilities must be carried out accurately to produce the outcome of 'Safe Medication Administration'.

Consider each 'gear' on the cover picture as a 'responsibility'. Each gear is dependent on the gear before it and the gear after it for the system to function; if one gear fails, the entire system fails. When all gears are functioning together, the result is a system that runs smoothly. Think of yourself as one of the gears; you will play an important role in the outcome of the medication system in your work location!

Learning about each responsibility in class and then applying what you have learned at your work location helps to promote the quality of life for the people you support as well as a safe work environment for you.

The following are your responsibilities as a MAP Certified staff:

- Observe and Report
- Assist with visits to the Health Care Provider (HCP)
- Obtain medication from the pharmacy
- Transcription
- Medication security
- Medication administration
- Documentation

This curriculum provides you with the details of each responsibility. It will continue to be a resource for you at your work location in your new role as a MAP Certified staff. Refer back to this curriculum often and practice what you are taught every day!

'Responsibilities in Action'

Content Writers:
Gina Hunt, RN and Carolyn Whittemore, RN

Content Developers:
Susan Canuel, RN; Mary Despres, RN; and Sharon Oxx, RN

Case Studies:
Mary Dewar, RN (Scott Green) and Carminda Jimenez, RN (Jonathan Brock)

Editors:
Marie Brunelle, RN; Bob Boyer, RN; Mary Dewar, RN; Lisa Kaliton, RN; Jo-Anne Shea, RN, Joanna Thomas, RN; Daniel Silva, RN; Heather Lake, RN and Matthew Meredith, RN

Contributors:
Claude Augustin, RN
Evelyn Brezniak, RN
David Bruno, RN
Pat Coupal, RN
Lori Gross, RN
Jackie Heard, RN
Tanya Jenkins, RN
Denise McGrath, RN
Denice Vignali, RN
Theresa Wolk, RN

Michele L. Deck, RN-use of a blank 12 box 'grid' as a teaching strategy

Reviewed and Approved by the Massachusetts Department of Public Health

The following training content may contain the trade names or trademarks of various third parties, and if so, any such use is solely for illustrative purposes only. All product and company names are trademarks™ or registered® trademarks of their respective holders. Use of them does not imply any affiliation with, endorsement by, or association of any kind between them and the Commonwealth of Massachusetts.

Initial release July 2017
Revised September 2020

Contents

Introduction 8
- MAP Certification 8
- MAP Recertification 9
- Where MAP Certification is Not Valid 10
- MAP Massachusetts Controlled Substance Registration (MCSR).............11
- MAP Policy Manual...11
- Symbols and their Meanings.......................................12
- Case Studies 13

Unit 1 Working at a MAP Registered Program 15

- Health Care Provider 15
- MAP Consultants 15
- Emergency Contacts 16
- Learning about the People You Support...........................17
- Principles of Medication Administration 18
  - Mindfulness 18
  - Supporting Abilities..18
  - Communication 18
- Respecting Rights...20

Unit 2 Observing and Reporting...23

- Observation 23
  - Objective Observation 23
  - Subjective Observation..24
- Reporting 24
  - Everyday Reporting 25
  - Immediate Reporting 26
- Documentation...29
  - How to Document...29
  - How to Correct a Documentation Error 30

Unit 3 Medications...32

- What are they? 32
- Brand and Generic...32
- Medication Categories 34
  - Controlled..34
  - Countable Controlled..35
  - Over-the-Counter (OTC)..38

Massachusetts | Responsibilities in Action   4

- Dietary Supplements 39
- Nutritional Supplements 39
- Medication Outcomes 42
  - Desired Effect 42
  - No Effect Noted 42
  - Side Effects 42
- Medication Interactions 43
- Alcohol, Nicotine and Caffeine 44
- Sensitivity to Medication 45
- Medication Information 45

Unit 4 Interacting with a Health Care Provider **48**

- Prepare the Person for the Appointment 48
  - Before Leaving the Program 48
- When You Get to the Appointment 50
  - During the Appointment 50
  - Advocate-Encourage Participation-Support Abilities 50
  - Obtain Signed/Dated HCP Order 50
    - Valid Orders 50
    - DMH/DCF Psychotropic Medication Orders 51
  - Obtain Prescription 52
  - Sample Medication 52
- After the Appointment 52
- People Who Manage Appointments Independently 55
- If Going to Emergency Room or Hospital 55
- Fax Health Care Provider Orders 57
- Telephone Health Care Provider Orders 57
- Exhausting a Current Supply of Medication 60

Unit 5 Obtaining, Storing and Securing Medication **64**

- Obtaining Medication 64
- Rogers Decision 68
- Pharmacy Label Components 69
- Ensure the Pharmacy Provided the Correct Medication 72
- When to Request a Medication Refill 73
- Tracking Medication 75
- Medication Storage and Security 76

Massachusetts | Responsibilities in Action   5

2020 The Massachusetts Departments of Public Health, Developmental Services, Mental Health, Children and Families and the Rehabilitation Commission

Unit 6 Recording Information 79

- Abbreviations 81
- The Medication Record 81
- Medication Sheet 82
- Transcribing a New HCP Order 95
- Discontinuing a Medication 96
- Posting and Verifying 103
- Medication Information Sheet 110

Unit 7 Administering Medications 111

- Regularly Scheduled Medications 111
- PRN Medications 112
- 5 Rights 116
  - Right Person 116
    - Emergency Fact Sheet 117
  - Right Medication 118
  - Right Dose 120
    - Dose = Strength X Amount 121
  - Right Time 123
  - Right Route 124
    - Routes Other than Oral 124
- 3 Checks 126
- Special Instructions 132
- Medication Administration Process 134
  - Prepare 134
    - Hand washing 134
  - Administer 135
  - Complete 136
- Medication Administration Process Checklist 137
- Medication Administration Process Visual 138
- Glove Use 139
- Do Not Administer Medication If 140
- Liquid Medication 141
  - Measuring Devices 145
- Medication Refusals 151
- Parameters 156
- Medication Ordered to be Held Before a Medical Test 158
- Medication is Not Available to Administer 159

Massachusetts | Responsibilities in Action 6

Unit 8 Chain of Custody **162**

- What 'Chain of Custody' Means 162
- Tracking Documents and Methods.. 163
  - o Medication Ordering and Receiving Log.. 164
  - o Pharmacy Receipts... 165
  - o Countable Controlled Substance Book... 166
    - Index 167
    - Count Sheets 169
    - Count Signature Sheets... 172
    - 'Shoulder to Shoulder' Count Procedure................................. 173
    - When and Why Two Signatures are Required 178
  - o Medication Sheets 180
    - Acceptable Codes.. 180
  - o Medication Release Document.. 183
    - Medication Transfer Form 184
  - o Medication Administration at other Locations 185
    - Day Program Medication and Residential Program Staff
      Responsibilities... 185
    - Day Program Staff Responsibilities.. 187
    - Off-Site Medication Administration... 190
    - Leave of Absence 195
  - o Disposal 200
  - o Blister Pack Monitoring 206
- Medication Supply Discrepancy 207

Unit 9 Medication Occurrences **214**

- Definition of a Medication Occurrence.. 214
- Definition of a Hotline Medication Occurrence.. 214
- Procedure Following a Medication Occurrence 215
- How to Help Minimize Medication Occurrences 217

Appendix.. **227**

Words You Should Know **245**

Answer Key **253**

Questions to Ask Your Supervisor... **276**

Massachusetts | Responsibilities in Action 7

Introduction

The Department of Public Health (DPH) serves as the lead agency for the Medication Administration Program (MAP) which is carried out jointly with the Department of Developmental Services (DDS), the Department of Mental Health (DMH), the Department of Children and Families (DCF) and the Massachusetts Rehabilitation Commission (MRC).

The overall goal of MAP is to ensure that there are appropriate policies and procedures for safe medication administration in MAP registered programs. This helps people receive their medication while living in the community and carrying on their day to day activities. The program makes it possible for direct support staff, who know the specific needs and concerns of each person, to administer medication as a part of the person's daily routine.

The Departments and the Commission allow direct support staff who has a current MAP Certificate to administer medication in:

- DDS adult residential, day and respite programs
- DMH/DCF adult and youth, day and respite programs
- MRC adult residential and day programs

These programs are registered with DPH. The MAP Certification is transferrable between DPH MAP registered programs only.

The in-person MAP Certification training program:
- Is a minimum of 16 hours in length
- Is taught by approved MAP Trainers
- Includes 3 pretest components
    1. Computer Based Test (CBT)
    o   Accessed at https://ma.tmuniverse.com/
        - On the TMU© homepage click 'Sign In'
        - Enter your log in information and click 'Sign In'
        - Click either the 'Test' tab at the top or the 'Testing' box
        - Under the 'Pretests' section click 'Begin Test'
        - Select an answer to each of the 30 questions in 35 minutes or less
        - Click 'End Test' to see your test results
        - Click 'Details' to see
            - Percentage (%) of questions you answered correctly
            - Topic of any question missed
                o   A test result of 80% or higher is 'passing'
    2. Medication Administration
        - Demonstration of process
            - Applying the 5 Rights as you complete the 3 Checks in 10 minutes or less
            - Feedback from MAP Trainer
    3. Transcription
        - Discontinue a medication and transcribe a new medication
            - 100% accuracy in 15 minutes or less

After you meet the CBT pretest requirement you are strongly encouraged to continue retaking the CBT pretest as many times as possible prior to your D&S Diversified Technologies CBT test date. There are over 200 questions in the database for you to answer. Retaking the CBT pretest many times along with reading the curriculum and reviewing all you will learn in your training will set you up for test success.

In preparation for the skills portions of the test, continue practicing transcriptions, paying close attention to the details. Practice the medication administration process using the medication administration demonstration video as a guide; available at www.hdmaster.com

Upon successful completion of the training program, you are eligible to schedule to take the MAP Certification test for a limited period of time.

MAP Certification is:

- Effective on the date that test results are posted on the D&S Diversified Technologies website at https://ma.tmuniverse.com/
- Valid for 2 years until the last day of the month in which you passed the test. For example, if you passed the test on July 6, 2020, your expiration date is July 31, 2022.

All DDS/DMH/DCF/MRC MAP registered programs are required to maintain acceptable proof of staff MAP Certification. A printout of your Massachusetts MAP Certification is available at:

https://ma.tmuniverse.com/

You are responsible for ensuring that your MAP Certification remains current.

Recertification must be completed every 2 years. To become recertified you must pass the recertification skills test.

If you do not pass the recertification test you may no longer administer medication. If you fail any combination of the recertification skills test (transcription or medication administration demonstration) components 3 times you must complete the full MAP Certification training program again and retake the CBT and skills tests.

You are encouraged to recertify before your MAP Certification expires. If your MAP Certification expires, you may no longer administer medication. You have one year to recertify. If you do not recertify within one year, you must complete the full MAP Certification training program again and retake the CBT and skills tests.

MAP Certification Is Not Valid for administration of medication to people who are under the age of 18 in DDS and MRC programs; nor is it valid at any of the following locations:

- Assisted Living Facilities
- Community-Based Acute Treatment (CBAT)
- Correctional Facilities
- Crisis Intervention Centers
- Day Habilitation
- Department of Youth Services
- Detoxification (Detox) Centers
- Home Care
- Hospitals
- Hospital Diversion Centers
- Intensive Community-Based Acute Treatment (ICBAT)
- Intensive Residential Treatment Programs (IRTP)
- Nursing Homes
- Rest Homes
- Schools (Public and Private)
- Stabilization Assessment and Rapid Reunification (STARR)
- Stabilization Programs
- In DDS, DMH, DCF and MRC programs not possessing a Massachusetts Controlled Substance Registration (MAP MCSR) from the Department of Public Health

Massachusetts | Responsibilities in Action

Massachusetts Controlled Substances Registration (MAP MCSR)

All eligible programs must be registered with the Department of Public Health. Proof of registration with DPH is the receipt of a MCSR number in the form of a certificate.

The MCSR allows medication to be stored at the program and authorizes MAP Certified staff to administer or assist in administration of medications. The MAP MCSR number begins with the letters 'MAP' followed by 5 numbers.

Throughout the training curriculum you will see this symbol indicating there is information specific to your work location that you must ask your Supervisor.

Ask your supervisor where the MAP MCSR certificate is placed in the medication area at your work location.

The MAP Policy Manual

Throughout the training curriculum you will see this symbol indicating there is additional information about a topic in the MAP Policy Manual. The MAP Policy Manual is a resource intended to provide service providers, trainers, staff and other interested parties with a single, topically organized source for MAP policies.

Each individual program registered with DPH must have a copy of the policy manual as part of the required reference materials for MAP Certified staff. The MAP Policy Manual is available at:

www.mass.gov/dph/map

Let's Begin!

Throughout the training curriculum you will see the word, year, abbreviated as 'yr' at the end of a date on Health Care Provider orders, pharmacy labels, medication administration sheets and medication progress notes. For training and testing purposes only, 'yr' represents the current year.

In addition you will find several symbols that identify important facts, indicate the need to seek more information about your work location or review information regarding policy and practice. When you see the following symbols you will know:

	There is information specific to your work location that you must ask your Supervisor
	There is additional information about the topic located in the MAP Policy Manual
	The information is important
	There is an exercise to complete
	The information that follows are important things to remember in the unit you just read

Case Studies

Juanita Gomez is a 36-year-old woman who uses facial expressions and nods her head yes or no when communicating her likes and dislikes. She has a seizure disorder that causes her to have uncontrolled, involuntary movements. She also has chronic muscle pain (contractures) currently managed with physical therapy and pain medication twice daily. She also has chronic constipation that is managed by keeping track of her bowel movements (BM) and administering bowel medication PRN (as needed.) She has difficulty swallowing (dysphagia) and requires supervision when eating or drinking. Juanita requires full assistance with activities of daily living (ADLs) including medication administration.

Ellen Tracey is a 42-year-old woman who communicates using simple words and short sentences. Her health issues include high blood pressure (hypertension) and high cholesterol (hyperlipidemia). Both are well controlled through diet and medication. Ellen also has an anxiety disorder; when anxious she bites her hands and slaps her head. Ellen's anxiety is managed with Ativan taken twice daily and once daily PRN. While staff is preparing her medications, Ellen will fill her glass with water.

Tanisha Johnson is a 22-year-old woman with a history of seizures following an acquired brain injury (ABI). Her seizures are well controlled with medication. Although she has an interest in learning about her medications and their possible side effects, she often refuses her medication. She enjoys going to her local health club and working with a trainer. She works at the local florist and goes to her family's home on weekends.

David Cook is a 52-year-old man with Down Syndrome. David is independent with ADLs and receives community based day supports. During day program hours, he participates in outings and volunteers in the community. In the evening David enjoys spending time with friends and family. At night David wears a continuous positive airway pressure device (C-PAP) to help keep his airway open due to sleep apnea (a potentially serious sleep disorder in which breathing repeatedly stops and starts). He is on several medications to treat high blood pressure, gastroesophageal reflux disease (GERD), swollen, painful joints (osteoarthritis) and a seizure disorder.

Scott Green is a 48-year-old man who has had multiple psychiatric hospitalizations. He is on several medications to treat schizophrenia, a mood disorder, high blood pressure, high cholesterol and non-insulin dependent diabetes (Type 2). He also takes PRN medication for headaches, heartburn and difficulty sleeping. Scott was interested in becoming more independent with his medications and in the past packed medication under staff supervision for up to two weeks at a time. However, he recently started not taking some of his medications on a regular basis. Staff have increased their support and now administers his medication. At his last psychiatric appointment staff reported that Scott preferred to take his medication in the evening. His doctor changed the timing of his medication from the morning to the evening.

Jonathan Brock is 6-year-old boy, with poor concentration and irritable behavior with angry outbursts. He is in kindergarten and receives significant support at school. His school utilizes a first/then schedule system with built in incentives. It was reported that his interest in activities such as playgroups and structured school activities had decreased. He has post-traumatic stress disorder (PTSD) and attention-deficit/hyperactivity disorder (ADHD); managed with medications.

When Jonathan began the medications for PTSD and ADHD, he struggled during administration time and would either spit out or refuse to take the medication. Staff would encourage and prompt him to take it, including putting the medication in applesauce and yogurt at the doctor's request. Jonathan told staff that he was refusing the medication because he was not able to swallow the tablets without choking. The psychiatrist changed the medication to a chewable form. Later when Jonathan started on a medication to help with sleep, it was ordered in liquid form. He completes daily living skills with staff support and prompts.

Unit 1

Working at a MAP Registered Program

Responsibilities you will learn

- Who will answer your medication and health related questions
- How you will get to know the people you support
- Medication administration principles
- Rights in relation to medication

Getting Your Medication and Health Related Questions Answered

A MAP Consultant is a valuable medication information resource. A MAP Consultant is:

- a registered nurse
- a registered pharmacist
- a Health Care Provider (HCP)
    - an authorized prescriber

An authorized prescriber is someone who is registered with the state of Massachusetts to prescribe medication.

Examples of authorized prescribers are a Health Care Provider (HCP), doctor, dentist, nurse practitioner, etc. For purposes of this training, an authorized prescriber is the same as a person's HCP.

Anytime you have health related questions contact the person's Health Care Provider.

MAP Consultants will help answer your questions about medication procedures, specific medication issues and what you should do next following the issue. When you call a MAP Consultant with your question, make sure you have the HCP order, the medication and the medication sheet available for reference; you may need to read them to the MAP Consultant.

Examples of when you need to contact a MAP Consultant include:

- too much or too little of a medication was administered
- the medication was omitted (not given)
- the HCP order, pharmacy label or medication sheet do not agree

Massachusetts | Responsibilities in Action

MAP Consultants are available 24 hours a day, 7 days a week. DPH requires that the telephone numbers for the MAP Consultants, poison control and other emergency numbers (911, fire, police) be clearly posted near the telephone in all programs.

This is an example of the emergency contact list in David Cook's home located near the phone for quick and easy staff reference.

Emergency Contact List

Rescue + Fire + Police
911

Poison Control
800-222-1222

MAP Consultants

Greenleaf Pharmacy
111-222-3434
Monday-Friday

Registered Nurse
Rebecca Long
781-000-4500
Saturday-Sunday

Health Care Provider(s)
Dr. Richard Black 617-332-0000
Dr. David Jones 617-332-0001
Dr. Shirley Glass 508-123-1234
Dr. Chen Lee 617-332-0002

Administrator on Duty
617-000-0000
Program Supervisor
Linda White
780-000-2222

Massachusetts | Responsibilities in Action

Ask your Supervisor where MAP Consultants, poison control and other emergency numbers are located in the program where you work.

Answer True (T) or False (F) if the person listed may act as a MAP Consultant.

1. ____ Licensed Practical Nurse (LPN)
2. ____ Pharmacy Technician
3. ____ Registered Nurse (RN)
4. ____ Receptionist at the HCP office
5. ____ Health Care Provider (HCP)
6. ____ MAP Certified Supervisor or Program Director
7. ____ Registered Pharmacist

Learning about the People You Support

Two of your most important responsibilities are watching for and reporting changes in the people you support. A change may be physical or behavioral. In order to recognize a change, you must first get to know the person by learning about their personality, physical conditions, abilities and medications. You can learn about a person who is new to you by:

- Observing (watching) the person
- Talking with the person
- Listening to the person
- Communicating with
    o the person's family
    o your co-workers
- Reading about the person's life and health history

Recognizing changes and reporting them to the right person will ensure the people you support will receive the best care possible.

Principles of Medication Administration

By following the principles of medication administration you will help to ensure medications are administered safely. The principles of medication administration are mindfulness, supporting abilities and communication.

- **Mindfulness**
  - Always remaining alert and focused during medication administration
  - Thinking about what you are doing and not something else
    - As you begin administering medication, you will very quickly become familiar with which person receives what medication at what time, etc. and even the size, shape, color and markings on the medication itself, because of this
      - Never allow medication administration to become routine
        - Consider changing the order of who you administer medications to first to help yourself to remain mindful.
- **Supporting abilities**
  - Helping the person to function as independently as possible
    - Encouraging a person to participate fully in the medication administration process based on their abilities

- **Communication**
  - Reading the HCP order, pharmacy label and medication sheet
    - Ensuring they agree
    - Contacting a MAP Consultant as needed
      - Informing your Supervisor after contacting a MAP Consultant
  - Talking and listening to the person while you are administering their medication

Communicating is a big part of your job. To communicate is to share or exchange information. In your role as a MAP Certified staff, you will communicate with the people you support, with your co-workers, supervisors, family members, the HCP, pharmacist, nurse and many others.

In addition to talking, communication also includes:

- Listening
- Documenting
- Body language
- Facial expression
- Tone of voice

For communication to be effective, remember:

- Speak clearly and slowly
- Look directly at the person you are speaking to
- Listen carefully
- Take notes during your shift if needed, this will help you with accurate documentation
- If information is given to you, repeat it back to the person to be sure you understood it correctly
- Ask questions if you do not understand something

Answer each question based on the case studies, and then write the related principle of medication administration (mindfulness, supporting abilities and communication).

1. Juanita takes her medication whole in pudding or applesauce. How would you know if she did not like a certain pudding flavor? _____
   What is the related principle? _____

2. How do you support Ellen's abilities during medication administration?
   _____
   What is the related principle? _____

3. Typically, you administer medications to the people in your work location in the same order each day. How can you ensure the medication administration process does not become routine? _____
   What is the related principle? _____

Massachusetts | Responsibilities in Action

Respecting Rights

Like you, the people you support have the right to be treated with both dignity and respect. Everyone also has the right to privacy. Confidentiality means keeping information private. Information about the people you support must only be shared with others if involved in their care.

In relation to medication administration, people have the right to

- know what their medications are and the reasons they are taken
- know the risks associated with taking the medication
- know the benefits associated with taking the medication
- refuse medication
- be given medication only as ordered by the HCP

If a person refuses to take their medication, the first thing you should do is ask them why they do not want to take it and report that information to the prescribing HCP and your supervisor. Ultimately, you want the people you support to receive their medications as ordered by the HCP. Until you know why the person is refusing their medications and report the issue, the problem cannot be solved.

The meaning of, a person has the right to be given medication only as ordered by the HCP, is shown in this example:

Ellen Tracey has an order for a PRN medication to manage her anxiety. You will only administer the medication when she displays symptoms of anxiety, as described in her HCP order and/or Support Plan. A Support Plan, if needed, is an extension of a HCP order. Although Ellen communicates using simple words and short sentences, she cannot tell you when she is anxious. Her plan describes in detail what you will observe when she experiences anxiety so that you will know exactly when to administer the medication. Administering PRN anti-anxiety medication for symptoms other than those described in her HCP order and/or Support Plan is not allowed.

At times, the instructions included in a HCP order regarding how and/or when to administer a medication are so lengthy that the order is written in the format of a Protocol or a Support Plan. A Protocol is typically seen when the reason the medication is ordered is to lessen a physical symptom, such as a seizure protocol, which gives instructions for the use of an anti-seizure medication when a person experiences a seizure. A Support Plan is typically seen when the reason the medication is ordered is to help lessen a behavior.

Support Plans and Protocols that reference medication are considered HCP orders.

Massachusetts | Responsibilities in Action

Ellen Tracey Support Plan
Anxiety Management
No Known Allergies

Specific symptoms that show us Ellen is anxious:

1. Biting hands for more than 4 minutes
2. Head slapping for longer than 30 seconds or more than 5 times in 4 minutes

   A. Staff will attempt to talk to Ellen in one on one conversation regarding current feelings and difficulties
   B. Staff will attempt to direct and involve Ellen in a familiar activity such as laundry, meal preparation, etc.

If unsuccessful with A and B, the Ativan may be administered.

Ativan 0.5mg once daily as needed by mouth; must give at least 4 hours apart from regularly scheduled Ativan doses. (Refer to HCP order)

If anxiety continues after the additional dose, notify HCP.

HCP signature: *Shirley Glass* MD 2/1/yr

Posted: **Sam Dowd 2-1-yr 4pm**
Verified: *Linda White 2-1-yr 4pm*

Review the support plan and answer the following questions.

1. What is the reason the PRN Ativan is ordered? _____

2. If Ellen was crying and attempted to hit you, could you administer the PRN Ativan? _____

3. What would you do if after the PRN medication was administered, Ellen continued slapping her head and biting her hands? _____

Let's Review

- Contact a person's HCP for health related issues, concerns or questions
- MAP Consultants are available 24 hours a day, 7 days a week to answer medication questions and/or provide technical assistance regarding medication
- MAP Consultants are a
  - HCP
  - Registered Pharmacist
  - Registered Nurse
- Your Supervisor must be informed anytime the MAP Consultant has been contacted
- To recognize changes, staff must learn about the people they support
- Medication Administration Principles include
  - Mindfulness
  - Supporting abilities
  - Communication
- Everyone has the right to be treated with dignity and respect

Unit 2

Observing and Reporting

Responsibilities you will learn

- The difference between objective and subjective observations
- When changes observed in a person should be reported
- How to accurately report the changes you observe
- How to correct a documentation error

Observation is the process of watching someone carefully in order to obtain information. You have such close day to day contact with the people you support; you will quickly become familiar with a person's daily routine, their habits, their likes and dislikes and may be the first staff to observe a change.

Observing, reporting and documenting physical and behavioral changes are your responsibility. These responsibilities are essential to the quality of the healthcare a person receives. Observations are either objective or subjective.

Objective observation is factual information you will see, hear, feel, smell or measure.

- See
  - Examples
    - Redness
    - Bruising
    - Scratch
    - Swelling
    - A person fall and bump their head

- Hear
  - Examples
    - Crying
    - Coughing
    - Sneezing
    - Moaning

- Feel
  - Examples
    - Warmth
    - Coolness
    - Dryness
    - Moist

- Smell
  - Examples

Massachusetts | Responsibilities in Action 23

- Body odor
- Halitosis (bad breath)
  - Measure
    - Examples
      - Number of hours a person sleeps
      - How long a seizure lasts
      - How much liquid a person drinks
      - How many pounds a person weighs
      - Vital Signs (blood pressure, temperature, pulse, respiration)

Subjective observation is when you work with a person who speaks or signs and they tell you how they are feeling.

- Examples
  - 'I have a headache'
  - 'My throat hurts'
  - 'I'm sad'
  - 'I'm tired'

Label each observation as objective (O) or subjective (S):

1. ___ Frowns getting off the van
2. ___ Limping
3. ___ David states he has 'sharp pain'
4. ___ Right knee is swollen, red and warm to touch
5. ___ David states 'My knee still hurts'

Reporting

Reporting is to give spoken or written information of something observed or told. You are responsible for reporting any changes, physical or behavioral, you notice. Report the facts. Do not guess at what you think the issue might be. The more details you report about what you see, hear, feel, smell or measure (objective observation) in addition to how the person says they are feeling (subjective observation) the better the HCP can determine the most appropriate treatment.

The quality of healthcare a person receives is only as good as the information you report to the HCP. When you report changes, follow up the next time you are working to see what action was taken.

When reporting physical and behavioral changes the expectation of who contacts the HCP varies from Provider to Provider, do you

- Call your Supervisor first for further directions?
- Contact the HCP directly, report the change, make an appointment if needed, and then call your Supervisor after?
- Contact someone else before your Supervisor?

Ask your Supervisor who is responsible for contacting the HCP to report changes observed in the people you support at your work location.

There are two types of reporting:

- **Everyday reporting**
- **Immediate reporting**

Everyday reporting typically occurs between staff present at shift change. Outgoing staff are expected to provide incoming staff with information in regard to basic household details such as a grocery list has been started as well as ongoing medication administration details they should be aware of and/or follow up on such as:

- 'PRN Ativan was administered to Ellen Tracey 30 minutes ago. Later in the shift, a medication progress note is needed documenting the response to the medication.'
- 'Tanisha Johnson went to the dentist today. Look at her HCP orders. An antibiotic was ordered. Her first dose will be at 4pm. The medication is a liquid and is locked in the refrigerator.'

Ask your Supervisor how information is shared between shifts; such as how new HCP orders are communicated if there is no staff present when you arrive for your shift.

Massachusetts | Responsibilities in Action   25

Immediate reporting is reporting without delay as soon as possible after a change is observed. Immediate reporting may prevent a small change observed from becoming a major health issue and allows the appropriate treatment to be ordered as quickly as possible.

Examples:
A runny nose could be a symptom of allergies or a symptom of a sinus infection.
A slight cough could be a symptom of a cold or a symptom of pneumonia (severe lung infection).

There are many people you will speak with to report information immediately, such as:

- 911 if

  - you are unsure a person is okay
  - a person falls and cannot get up
  - a person complains of chest pain, has difficulty breathing or is choking
  - a person is unresponsive
  - a MAP Consultant recommends you hang up and call 911
  - directed by a current HCP order or Protocol
    - For example:
      - A HCP order or Protocol states, 'Call 911 for seizure activity greater than 5 minutes.'

- Poison control when a

  - person ingests a foreign substance such as laundry detergent
  - MAP Consultant recommends you hang up and call poison control

- A MAP Consultant when

  - an occurrence (error) is made when administering medication
    - For example:
      - Tegretol 400mg is ordered and Tegretol 600mg is administered
  - the medication received from the pharmacy seems different from the HCP order
    - Even if other staff have administered it
  - you notice the medication is different in color, size, shape and/or markings from the last time it was obtained
  - you are not able to administer the medication based on the strength of medication received from the pharmacy
    - For example:
      - The dose ordered is 50mg and you receive a 100mg strength tablet from the pharmacy

Massachusetts | Responsibilities in Action   26

- The HCP who prescribed medication when

  - medication is refused
  - medication is not available from the pharmacy
  - there are no refills left
  - a medication parameter (guideline) for HCP notification has been met
    - For example:
      - A HCP order states, 'If pulse is below 56, do not give the medication and contact the HCP.'
  - a MAP Consultant recommends you hang up and call the HCP
  - an order is missing the person's name, medication, dose, frequency, route or the date and the HCP signature

- Your Supervisor when

  - there is a math error in the Countable Controlled Substance Book
    - typically known as a Count Book
  - the count signature pages in a Count Book are almost full
  - the Count Book binding is loose
  - a medication seems to be tampered with
  - the medication supply is low and you are unsure if a refill has been ordered
  - you cannot locate a medication to administer

A Countable Controlled Substance Book, a method used to track certain medications, is typically referred to as a Count Book. For training purposes, the term Count Book will be used.

Make sure all of your questions are answered by the person you contacted and document the conversation including

- your question or concern
- the response given to you
- the name of the person you contacted
- date, time and your full name

Massachusetts | Responsibilities in Action   27

Review the narrative note regarding David's knee pain.

\multicolumn{3}{c	}{**NARRATIVE NOTES**}	
Name of Individual	\multicolumn{2}{l	}{David Cook}	
DATE	**TIME**	**NARRATIVE** Include observations, communications, information sharing, HCP visits, medication changes, changes from the familiar, etc.	**STAFF SIGNATURE**
3/3/yr	3PM	David frowns getting off the van today, is limping and states he has 'sharp pain' when bending his knee. His right knee is now swollen, red and warm to touch.	John Craig
3/3/yr	3:15PM	Ibuprofen 400mg was given for complaint of 'sharp knee pain'. Call made to Dr. Black and message left.	John Craig
3/3/yr	4:15pm	David received Ibuprofen 400mg at 3:15 PM and still complains of right knee pain. Even though Ibuprofen has been given as ordered, his symptoms continue.	Sam Dowd
3/3/yr	4:45pm	Dr. Black returned call, no medication changes but would like to see David tomorrow, appointment made for 2 PM.	Sam Dowd

Place a checkmark next to the most complete information to report to the HCP.

1. ___ David's osteoarthritis has been bothering him. His knee is red, swollen and painful. He has received Ibuprofen for the pain.

2. ___ David has injured his knee. He is limping because his knee hurts; it is red, swollen and warm to touch.

3. ___ David has received Ibuprofen and states his right knee still hurts. It is warm to touch, red and swollen. He is limping.

4. ___ David states he has, 'sharp pain' when he bends his right knee. He frowns getting off the van and is limping. His right knee is now red, warm to touch and swollen. He has received Ibuprofen 400mg for right knee pain and his symptoms continue.

Documentation

Documentation should tell a story from beginning to end whether an issue takes a day, many days or weeks to resolve.

When documenting:

- Use blue or black ink
- Write
  - Clearly
  - In complete sentences
- Include
  - Date
  - Time
  - Your full name

You will be documenting medication administration on the front side of a medication administration sheet; however, there are times when additional documentation is required.

Additional medication related documentation is typically written on a medication progress note form; usually on the backside of a medication administration sheet. Medication progress notes are kept in a medication book. When documenting using a medication progress note, use as many lines as needed.

Name Juanita Gomez   **MEDICATION PROGRESS NOTE**

Date	Time	Medication	Dose	Given	Not Given	Refused	Other	Reason (for giving/not giving)	Results and/or Response	Staff Signature
3/3/yr	8:27pm	Magnesium Hydroxide	1200mg	X				Third day with no BM		Serena Wilson
3/3/yr	11pm	No BM as of 11pm. Night staff will continue to monitor.								Serena Wilson
3/4/yr	8:42am	No BM overnight. Dr. Jones notified. Telephone order taken to give Magnesium Hydroxide 1200mg tonight if there is still no BM by 8pm. If the medication is administered and there is still no BM, call Dr. Jones tomorrow morning. See HCP order.								_Timothy Miller_
3/4/yr	3:31pm	Had a large ~~bowl~~ (error SW) bowel movement.								Serena Wilson

2020 The Massachusetts Departments of Public Health, Developmental Services, Mental Health, Children and Families and the Rehabilitation Commission

If a health issue is chronic (ongoing) such as constipation for which there is a PRN medication prescribed, documentation in the medication progress notes helps keep track of how often the PRN medication is needed and if it has any effect.

This is key information for a HCP, for example, if the HCP knows that Juanita is receiving PRN Magnesium Hydroxide on an ongoing basis over a period of time, a daily bowel medication may be considered in an effort to reduce PRN Magnesium Hydroxide use.

You may work in a location that uses a separate form to document additional medication information instead of a medication progress note form. In this situation, additional medication or health related documentation may be written on progress notes, sometimes called narrative notes, which are filed in the person's confidential health record.

NARRATIVE NOTES

Name of Individual		Juanita Gomez	
DATE	TIME	**NARRATIVE** Include observations, communications, HCP visits, medication changes, changes from the familiar, reportable events, etc.	STAFF SIGNATURE
3-3-yr	8:27pm	Magnesium Hydroxide 1200mg administered at 8pm since third day with no BM. ———————————————————————————	Serena Wilson
3-3-yr	11pm	No results as of 11pm. Night staff will continue to monitor.	Serena Wilson
3-4-yr	8:42am	No bowel movement overnight. Dr. Jones notified. Telephone order taken to give Magnesium Hydroxide 1200mg again just tonight if there is still no BM by 8pm. If the medication is administered and there is still no BM, call Dr. Jones tomorrow morning. See HCP order. ———————————	*Timothy Miller*
3-4-yr	3:31pm	Large ~~bowl~~ (error SW) bowel movement. —————————	Serena Wilson

Medication sheets, medication progress notes, narrative notes and HCP orders, etc. are legal documents. If you make a documentation error, never use 'white-out', mark over or erase the error; this can be viewed as an attempt to hide something.

To correct a documentation error:
- Draw a single line through the error
- Write 'error'
- Write your initials
  - Then document what you meant to write the first time
    - For example, see the medication progress note and/or the narrative note entries dated 3-4-yr at 3:30pm

Let's Review

- Knowing the people you support will help you recognize when there is a change
- Subjective information is what a person tells you
- Objective information can be seen, heard, felt, smelled or measured
- All changes must be reported
- Reporting immediately decreases the chances a health issue may become worse
- A HCP uses the information reported by staff to determine if treatment and medication are needed
- Health related issues are documented from beginning to end

Unit 3

Medications

Responsibilities you will learn

- The purpose of medications
- Medication categories
- Medication outcomes
- Medication information resources

Medications are substances that when put into or onto the body will change one or more ways the body works. Medications are used to treat illness, disease, pain or behavior. When a medication is prescribed the goal is that the person's symptoms will lessen and their quality of life will improve.

You will learn how to administer medications safely, following the same steps each time you administer a medication; this will help you to safely administer medication to the people you support.

Brand and Generic

Medications are known by their brand name and/or generic name. Typically, all medications have a brand and a generic name.

Brand name medications are created and made by a specific pharmaceutical company. When a pharmaceutical company creates a medication they are allowed to name it. Examples of brand name medications are Tylenol, Advil and Prozac.

Generic medications are known by their chemical name and are manufactured by many different pharmaceutical companies. Generic medication is similar to its brand name medication but is less expensive; the name is different and may have a different color, marking, shape and/or size. Examples of generic name medications are Acetaminophen, Ibuprofen and Fluoxetine.

When the HCP submits a prescription for a brand name medication and the generic medication is supplied by the pharmacy, you will see the generic name of the medication and the letters 'IC' near the brand name of the medication printed on the pharmacy label.

'IC' is an abbreviation for 'interchange'. This means the generic name medication was supplied by the pharmacy in place of the brand name medication.

Review the pharmacy labels. Fill in the generic medication supplied.

Zestril _____   Prilosec _____   Motrin _____

Rx#138   **Greenleaf Pharmacy**   111-222-3434
             20 Main Street
             Treetop, MA 00000   1/31/yr
David Cook

Lisinopril 20 mg   Qty. 60
IC Zestril

Take 2 tablets by mouth one time a day in the morning.
Hold if systolic blood pressure is below 100 and notify HCP.

                                      Dr. Black
Lot# 269   ED: 1/31/yr   Refills: 2

Rx#174   **Greenleaf Pharmacy**   111-222-3434
             20 Main Street
             Treetop, MA 00000   6/30/yr
David Cook

Omeprazole 20 mg   Qty. 30
IC Prilosec

Take 1 tablet by mouth once a day before supper

                                      Dr. Black
Lot# 1436   ED: 6/30/yr   Refills: 2

Rx#140   **Greenleaf Pharmacy**   111-222-3434
             20 Main Street
             Treetop, MA 00000   8/31/yr
David Cook

Ibuprofen 400 mg   Qty. 90
IC Motrin

Take 1 tablet by mouth every eight hours as needed for right knee pain.
If symptoms continue for more than 48 hours notify HCP.

                Dr. Black
Lot# 745   ED: 8/31/yr   Refills: 2

Medication Schedules

All prescription medications are known as controlled substances. This means a prescription from a HCP is required to obtain the medication from a pharmacy.

Controlled substances are placed into schedules. The schedules are numbered; II, III, IV, V and VI. The schedule a substance is placed in is based on its abuse potential, and when abused, its chance of causing dependence.

Medication Categories

There are three categories of medications:

- **Controlled (Schedule VI)**
- **Countable Controlled (Schedule II-V)**
- **Over-the-Counter (OTC)**

Controlled (Schedule VI) Medication

Controlled medications require a prescription, submitted by the HCP, in order to obtain the medication from a pharmacy. The pharmacist uses the information on the prescription to prepare and label the medication. Examples of controlled medications include antibiotics (Amoxicillin), antidepressants (Prozac) and antipsychotics (Haldol).

Controlled medication requirements include:

- A HCP order for administration
- Labeled and packaged by the pharmacy
  - In a bottle or
  - May be in a tamper resistant package
- Secured in a key locked area
- Tracked using a
  - Medication Ordering/Receiving log
  - Medication sheet
    - Where the medication is documented after administration
  - Medication Release Document
  - DPH Disposal Record

Additional training and documentation is required specific to certain 'high alert' controlled medications as identified by DPH. High alert medications include Coumadin and Clozaril (schedule VI).

Massachusetts | Responsibilities in Action

Ask your supervisor if anyone has HCP orders for 'high alert' medication at your work location.

DPH periodically identifies some Schedule VI medications as having a 'high risk' for abuse potential, with the expectation they be tracked closely as if they were a countable controlled medication.

Ask your supervisor if anyone has HCP orders for 'high risk' for abuse Schedule VI medication at your work location and if so, how they are tracked.

Countable Controlled Medication (Schedule II-V)

Schedule II-V substances are sometimes called narcotics. Examples of countable controlled medications include prescription pain relievers (Percocet, Vicodin) or antianxiety medication (Ativan).

Due to the high risk for these medications to be stolen and abused, countable controlled medications have additional security measures in place.

Countable controlled medications require a prescription, written by the HCP, in order to obtain the medication from a pharmacy. The pharmacist uses the information on the prescription to prepare and label the medication.

The pharmacy must also add an 'identifier' on the package of the countable controlled medication to alert you to the fact that it is a countable controlled medication, such as a 'C' stamped on the package, an Rx (prescription) number that may start with a 'C' or an 'N' or the package itself may be color coded.

Pharmacy 'identifier' examples:

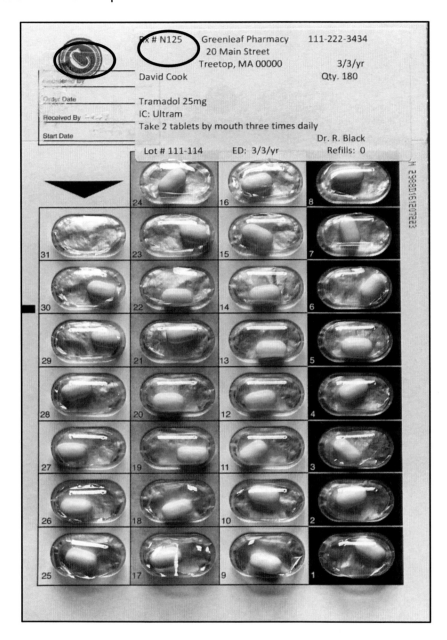

Ask your supervisor how the pharmacy identifies countable controlled medication at your work location.

In the event the pharmacy has no obvious identifier, the pharmacist must be contacted for assistance in determining which medications delivered are countable controlled.

Countable controlled medication requirements include:

- A HCP order for administration
- Labeled and packaged by the pharmacy in a
  - Tamper resistant package
    - The reason for this type of packaging is to decrease the chance that the medication inside is replaced with a different medication
    - With an identifier
- Secured in a double key locked area
  - A key lock within a key lock
    - The reason for a double key locked storage area is to maintain medication security
- Tracked using a
  - Medication Ordering/Receiving log
  - Count Book
    - Added into a Count Book as medications come into the program
    - Subtracted from a Count Book as medications are removed from the package or transferred
  - Medication sheet
    - Where the medication is documented after administration
  - Medication Release Document
  - DPH Disposal Record
- Counted every time the medication storage keys change hands
  - Counting this frequently ensures medications are secure and
    - Protects you from being accused of mishandling or misusing medication
    - Assists you in adhering to laws, regulations and policies

If controlled substances, countable controlled substances or the paper copy of prescriptions are stolen, an investigation will follow with probable police involvement.

Over-the-Counter (OTC) Medication

Over-the-Counter (OTC) or nonprescription medication may be purchased from a pharmacy without a prescription from the HCP; however, MAP requires that all OTC medications be labeled by the pharmacy. This means that you must ask the HCP to submit a prescription for all OTC medications so that the pharmacy will prepare and label the medication. Examples of OTC medications include nonprescription pain relievers (Tylenol, Advil) or allergy medication (Benadryl).

OTC medication requirements include:
- A HCP order for administration
- Packaged by the pharmacy
  - In a bottle or may be in a
  - Tamper resistant package
- Labeled by the pharmacy
- Secured in a key locked area
- Tracked using a
  - Medication Ordering/Receiving log
  - Medication sheet
    - Where the medication is documented after administration
  - Medication Release Document

Sunscreen, insect repellant and personal hygiene cleansing products do not require a HCP order.

In addition to the three categories of medications there are Dietary Supplements.

Dietary Supplements

Dietary supplements are products that contain dietary ingredients such as vitamins, minerals, herbs or other substances. Unlike medication, dietary supplements are not pre-approved by the government for safety or effectiveness before marketing. Dietary supplements may be purchased from a pharmacy without a prescription from the HCP however; MAP requires that all dietary supplements be labeled by the pharmacy, with some possible exceptions. This means that you must ask the HCP to submit a prescription for all dietary supplements so that the pharmacy will prepare and label the supplement. Examples include Multivitamins, Fish Oil and Shark Cartilage.

Dietary supplement requirements include:
- A HCP order for administration
- Packaged by the pharmacy
  - In a bottle or may be in a
  - Tamper resistant package
- Labeled by the pharmacy
- Secured in a key locked area
- Tracked using a
  - Medication Ordering/Receiving log
  - Medication sheet
    - Where the medication is documented after administration
  - Medication Release Document

Nutritional Supplements

Nutritional supplements are 'conventional' food items such as Ensure, gastric tube feedings or Carnation Instant Breakfast; they are not medications and do not fall under MAP. Although nutritional supplements do not fall under MAP, the use of such products is typically tracked on various types of forms.

For your general information, to know if a product is an OTC medication, a dietary supplement or a nutritional supplement, look at the manufacturer's label.

Over-the-counter medications have a Drug Facts label.

Dietary Supplements have a Supplement Facts label.

'Conventional' Foods have a Nutrition Facts label.

Look at the manufacturer's label for each product. Determine if the product is an OTC medication, dietary supplement or nutritional supplement and answer the corresponding questions.

1. This product is a(n)
   a. Dietary Supplement
   b. OTC Medication
   c. Nutritional Supplement

2. Is a HCP order required for administration? _____

3. Is a pharmacy label required for administration? _____

4. Is the product transcribed onto a medication sheet? __

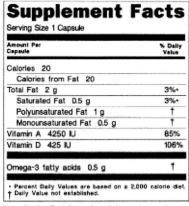

1. This product is a(n)
   a. Dietary Supplement
   b. OTC Medication
   c. Nutritional Supplement

2. Is a HCP order required for administration? _____

3. Is a pharmacy label required for administration? _____

4. Is the product transcribed onto a medication sheet? __

Massachusetts | Responsibilities in Action

Medication Outcomes

What happens or does not happen after a medication is administered is known as a medication outcome. When a medication is given it may cause any of the following outcomes:

- **Desired Effect**
- **No Effect Noted**
- **Side Effects**

Desired effect is when a medication does exactly what it was intended to do; the person experiences the beneficial results of the medication. For example: Tylenol is administered for a headache and the headache goes away or Dilantin is administered to control seizures and the person is seizure free.

No effect noted is when a medication is taken for a specific reason and the symptoms continue; no effects are noted from the medication. This could occur for one of two reasons.

1. The body will not respond to the medication and a different medication will need to be ordered. For example, Erythromycin is ordered for an ear infection; the person has ear pain and a temperature of 100.2, after taking the medication for 2 days the person still has the same symptoms; ear pain and a temperature of 100.2. No effect was noted from the medication, the person continues to experience symptoms and the HCP must be notified.

2. The medication has not had enough time to work. For example, a person was started on a new antidepressant medication a week ago and is still experiencing symptoms of depression. Some medications take longer to work than other medications; in this case several weeks may be necessary for the person's symptoms to improve.

When a new medication is started, you should document what you observe, even if there are no effects noted. This will help the HCP in determining if the medication is working as intended.

Side effects are results from a medication that were not wanted or intended even if the desired effect is achieved. Side effects are usually mild, and while they may be uncomfortable, are usually not severe enough for the HCP to discontinue the medication. For example, an antibiotic may cure an ear infection but it may also cause mild nausea, or a cold medicine may reduce a cough and runny nose but may also cause sleepiness.

Side effects range from minor to severe. If the side effect is more severe, it is called an adverse response to the medication. For example, if an antibiotic caused diarrhea and vomiting, the HCP may consider discontinuing that medication and ordering a different one.

Adverse responses (severe side effects) to observe for include:

- **Allergic reaction:** the body's immune system reacts to the medication as if it were a foreign substance. An allergic reaction is usually characterized by a rash which may start on the chest, spread to the back, arms and then down the body, to the legs. An allergic reaction may happen at any time, even if the person has taken the medication in the past.

- **Anaphylactic reaction:** a severe, very dangerous, life threatening allergic reaction. An anaphylactic reaction happens very quickly and requires immediate medical attention, such as calling 911. An anaphylactic reaction is usually characterized by difficulty breathing, rash and changes in vital signs.

- **Paradoxical reaction:** when the response the person experiences is opposite of what the medication was intended to produce. For example, a medication is ordered to help a person relax and instead the person becomes restless.

- **Toxicity:** when a medication builds up in the body to the point where the body cannot handle it anymore; this can be life threatening. Toxicity is more common with certain medications than others. For example, even a very common medication, such as Tylenol, can be toxic. Many anti-seizure medications also have the ability to build up in the body causing toxicity. Typically, a person's blood will be monitored for medication levels to ensure they are not toxic.

Medication Interactions

A medication interaction is a mixing of medications in the body which will either increase or decrease the effects and/or side effects of one or both of the medications; the more medications a person takes the greater the possibility of an interaction occurring. In addition to medications interacting with each other, medications can also interact with dietary supplements, other substances and certain foods.

Examples of medication interactions:
- If an antibiotic is taken with Calcium, the Calcium interacts with the antibiotic decreasing the effects of the antibiotic; this means the person will not get the beneficial result from the antibiotic.
- Vitamin K, often found in leafy green vegetables, interacts with Warfarin Sodium (a blood thinner) decreasing the effects of the Warfarin Sodium; this means the person will not get the beneficial result (for the blood to be thinned) from the Warfarin Sodium.
- If more than one pain medication is taken at a time, they can interact increasing the effects and/or side effects of either pain medication.

Alcohol, Nicotine and Caffeine

Substances such as alcohol, nicotine and caffeine have the ability to interact or interfere with the absorption of medication in the body. You must inform the HCP if any of the people you support use these substances.

Read the interactions section of the Tramadol medication information sheet. Circle what could happen if Tramadol is taken with an alcoholic drink.

Sample Medication Information Sheet

Tramadol: is an analgesic used to treat moderate to severe pain, chronic pain. Brand names for Tramadol are Conzip, Rybix, Ryzolt, Ultram, and Zytram

How to take: Oral tablets, take with or without food.

What to do if you miss a dose: Take as soon as possible unless it is one hour before the next dose. If so, skip the missed dose. Never double up on dose.

Side Effects: Vertigo, depression, seizures, headache, fatigue, hypotension, blurred vision, nasal congestion, nausea, anorexia, constipation, GI irritation, diarrhea, pruritus and urinary retention.

Interactions: Tell your HCP of all the medications you are taking. Do not use with St. John's Wort. Using Tramadol together with alcohol may increase side effects such as dizziness, drowsiness, confusion, and difficulty concentrating.

Contraindications: Hypersensitivity, acute intoxication with any CNS depressant, alcohol, asthma, respiratory depression.

Special Precautions: Monitor vital signs, if respirations are less than 12 withhold, track bowels, and check urinary output.

Overdose reaction: Serotonin syndrome, neuroleptic malignant syndrome: increased heart rate, sweating, dilated pupils, tremors, high B/P, hyperthermia, headache, and confusion.

Massachusetts | Responsibilities in Action

Sensitivity to Medication

Each person may respond differently to the same medication. How a person responds depends on how sensitive they may or may not be to the medication. There are several factors that contribute to a person's sensitivity to medication.

These factors include:
- Age
- Weight
- Gender
- General health
- Medical history
- Level of physical activity
- Use of other medications or dietary supplements

For example, a HCP would not necessarily order the same medication or dose of medication for a 100 pound woman as he would for a 275 pound man or a healthy 25 year old and an 85 year old with many health issues.

Medication Information

You are responsible to learn about the medications you administer and know the reason for administration. To monitor the person for effects of medication you must

- learn about the people you support including their medical conditions and medications prescribed
- read about each new medication before administering
- know where to find or how to contact medication information resources

Resources for medication information include

- the MAP Consultant
- the medication information sheet
  - supplied by the pharmacy for each medication prescribed
- a reputable online source
- a drug reference book

Ask your supervisor where the current (less than 2 years old) drug reference book (paperback or hardcover) and/or the current (less than 2 years old) printed medication information sheets for all prescribed medications are located in the program where you work.

Match the terms to the corresponding examples or actions required.

1. ___ Controlled Medication — A Mild itching and rash occur after taking a new medication

2. ___ Medication Sensitivity — B A prescription is required to obtain it but does not require counting; schedule VI medication

3. ___ Anaphylactic Reaction — C A 100 pound person becomes very sleepy after receiving a normal dose of Ibuprofen

4. ___ No Effect Noted — D Coumadin and Aspirin taken together cause a person's gums to bleed

5. ___ Dietary Supplement — E Medication is ordered to help calm a person, instead the person becomes restless

6. ___ Paradoxical Effect — F Must be counted every time the keys change hands

7. ___ Countable Medication — G Immediate 911 call required

8. ___ Toxicity — H Mild upset stomach after receiving an antibiotic

9. ___ Side Effect — I Tylenol is taken for back pain and the back pain goes away

10. ___ Desired Effect — J The body stores up more medication than it can handle

11. ___ Allergic Reaction — K Multivitamin

12. ___ Medication Interaction — L An antibiotic is ordered for bronchitis; after 2 days the person is still coughing and has a fever

Let's Review

- A medication has the ability to change one or more ways the body works
- Medications are known by their brand name and/or generic name
- Categories of medications are:
  - Controlled (Schedule VI)
  - Countable Controlled (Schedule II-V)
  - Over-the-Counter (OTC)
- Medication outcomes include:
  - desired effect
  - no effect noted
  - side effects
- Adverse responses are severe side effects
- Medications and dietary supplements have the ability to interact with each other, alcohol, nicotine, caffeine and certain foods, either increasing or decreasing the effect of the medication or dietary supplement or both
- The more medications and dietary supplements a person takes the greater the possibility of an interaction
- A HCP order is required to administer all medications and dietary supplements
- You are responsible to learn about the medications you administer
- You are responsible to know the reason a medication is ordered

Unit 4

Interacting with a Health Care Provider

Responsibilities you will learn

- A procedure to help ensure a successful HCP visit
- When medication reconciliation is required
- The process of taking a telephone order
- What is required to use an existing supply of medication when there is a dose or a frequency change

Sometimes the changes you observe and report result in a HCP visit. There will be times when you will go with a person for a particular problem, issue or concern that you, other staff or the person want to discuss with the HCP or for their routine yearly physical examination.

A procedure to ensure that you are prepared with all the information and forms needed when accompanying a person to a medical appointment is as follows:

Prepare the Person for the Appointment

- Tell the person the date and time, when appropriate
- Discuss what is going to happen at the visit
- Follow any instructions ordered to prepare for the visit
  - For example
    - Pre-medications ordered prior to the appointment
    - Fasting, such as no food or fluid prior to the appointment
- Think About
  - Items to keep the person occupied
  - Encouraging the person to wear loose and comfortable clothing in the event the HCP needs to physically examine the person

Before leaving the program, make sure you have the following:

- Person's insurance card
- Copy of current medication sheets or a list of medications
- HCP Encounter/Consult/Order Form
  - The top portion is completed by program staff
    - Name of person
    - Date
    - Allergies
    - Reason(s) for visit
    - List of current medication, including dietary supplements and PRNs
    - Name of HCP
    - Signature of staff person completing the form

Massachusetts | Responsibilities in Action   48

HEALTH CARE PROVIDER ORDER

Name: David Cook	**Date:** June 1, yr
Health Care Provider: Dr. Black	**Allergies:** No Known Allergies
Reason for Visit: David states that he has burning in his throat after eating.	
Current Medications: Zestril 40 mg by mouth once a day in the morning. Check blood pressure before administering medication. If systolic reading is less than 100, hold medication and notify HCP. Motrin 400 mg by mouth as needed every 8 hours for right knee pain. Notify HCP if right knee pain continues for more than 48 hours.	
Staff Signature: *Sam Dowd*	**Date:** June 1, yr
Health Care Provider Findings:	
Medication/Treatment Orders:	
Instructions:	
Follow-up visit:	**Lab work or Tests:**
Signature:	**Date:**

Staff Complete Top of Form

HCP Completes Bottom of Form

Posted by: Date: Time: Verified by: Date: Time:

Each department, DDS, DMH, DCF and MRC uses standardized forms and/or tools or the forms used have required information that must be included relating to a HCP visit.

Ask your Supervisor what HCP visit forms are required specific to the people you support.

If another staff completes the paperwork, make sure you read it before leaving so you can tell the HCP why the visit was needed when you are asked.

Make sure you also have:

- Driving directions
- Money for parking, gas, food or drink
- Provider on-call information (in case you need to contact someone)
- Family/Guardian information
- Name of the pharmacy, telephone number and directions
- A charged cell phone

When You Get to the Appointment

- First, check in with the receptionist
  - Introduce yourself and the person you are accompanying
  - State the reason that you are there i.e. 'David Cook has a 2pm appointment to see Dr. Black'
  - Discuss any accommodations the person may need in the waiting room

During the Appointment

- Assist the person, if needed
- Advocate, encourage participation and support abilities
  - Provide HCP Encounter/Consult/Order and other forms
  - Provide information to the HCP when asked
  - Communicate the reason for the visit
    - This is especially important when the person does not speak
  - If the person can speak about their health encourage them to do so
  - Redirect the HCP to the person you are assisting when the HCP asks questions so that they may answer whenever possible
    - Help the person to answer questions, if needed
  - Ask the HCP for answers to any questions the person or you have
  - Write down any information that is given to you that is not on the forms so that it can be communicated to others after the appointment

Obtain the Written Results and Recommendations of the Appointment including:

- HCP Encounter/Consult/Order Form
  - Make sure the HCP's portion of the form is completed
    - HCP orders must include:
      - The 5 rights of medication administration

- - Person's name
    - Medication name
    - Dose
    - Frequency
    - Route
  - Allergies
  - HCP findings
  - Special Instructions, if any
  - Target signs and symptoms, instructions and/or parameters for PRN medication
  - Acceptable HCP signatures:
    - A 'wet' signature
      - The order is signed with pen and ink by the HCP
    - An 'image' of the HCP's signature
    - An 'electronic' signature
      - When orders are received, unaltered through an electronic system
        - only the last page of the HCP order needs to be (electronically) signed and dated by the HCP and
        - all HCP order pages must be fastened together as one packet.
  - Date of the order, including the year

HCP orders, including Protocols/Support Plans are valid for 1 year, typically corresponding to an annual physical during a HCP visit. If the physical cannot be scheduled before the order expires, the order is valid until the day after the annual HCP visit occurs, as long as:

- A person's health insurance plan requires a certain amount of time between annual physicals, such as one year and one day; and
- Staff made an effort to obtain an appointment with the HCP on the earliest possible date allowed by the insurance company.

In DMH and DCF only, psychotropic medication orders must be updated at clinically appropriate intervals as determined by the prescribing HCP.

PRN medication orders must include specific target signs and symptoms and instructions for use including what to do if the medication is given and is not effective.

Massachusetts | Responsibilities in Action

- Prescription
    - The HCP may
        - submit the prescription electronically to the pharmacy
        - call the prescription into the pharmacy
        - give the prescription to
            - you to bring to the pharmacy
            - the person to bring to the pharmacy, if self-administering
    - If given a written prescription ensure it and the HCP order agree before leaving
        - Both must include the 5 rights of medication administration

- Sample medication may be received from a HCP and administered if the HCP labels the sample medication with the same information as on a pharmacy label and includes the HCP's name and writes a HCP order for the sample medication
- Set up another appointment with the receptionist, if needed

 Prescriptions may not be used in place of a HCP order.

After the Medical Appointment

- Ensure the pharmacy received the prescription
- Pick up new medications at the pharmacy or check on when the pharmacy will deliver the medication
- Bring back all forms, any prescriptions, HCP orders, and the next appointment card to give to the appropriate person
- Transcribe all medication orders on to the medication administration sheet
    - Post and Verify all orders
- Secure the medication
- Document the visit
- Communicate changes to all staff

Review the HCP order below and fill in the blanks.

HEALTH CARE PROVIDER ORDER

Name: David Cook	**Date:** June 1, yr
Health Care Provider: Dr. Black	**Allergies:** No Known Allergies
Reason for Visit: David states that he has burning in his throat after eating.	
Current Medications: Zestril 40 mg by mouth once a day in the morning. Check blood pressure before administering medication. If systolic reading is less than 100, hold medication and notify HCP. Motrin 400 mg by mouth as needed every 8 hours for right knee pain. Notify HCP if right knee pain continues for more than 48 hours.	
Staff Signature: *Sam Dowd*	**Date:** June 1, yr
Health Care Provider Findings: Gastroesophageal reflux disease (GERD)	
Medication/Treatment Orders: Prilosec 20 mg by mouth once a day before supper	
Instructions: remain upright 30 minutes after eating	
Follow-up visit: 1 month	**Lab work or Tests:** None today
Signature: *Richard Black, MD*	**Date:** June 1, yr

Posted by: Date: Time: Verified by: Date: Time:

1. HCP name   _____
2. Reason for visit   _____
3. Staff completing form   _____
4. Allergies   _____
5. HCP findings   _____
6. New medication ordered   _____
7. HCP instructions   _____

Tanisha went to the dentist today. She received a new order for an antibiotic. You return to Tanisha's home with a signed HCP order. Review the HCP order and complete the following exercise.

HEALTH CARE PROVIDER ORDER

Name: Tanisha Johnson	**Date:** Feb. 2, yr
Health Care Provider: Dr. Chen Lee	**Allergies:** No known medication allergies
Reason for Visit: Complaining of soreness in back of mouth.	
Current Medications: Phenobarbital 64.8mg once daily in the evening by mouth Clonazepam 1mg twice daily at 8am and 4pm by mouth	
Staff Signature: *Sam Dowd*	**Date:** Feb. 2, yr
Health Care Provider Findings: Inflammation of gum-line on left side of mouth	
Medication/Treatment Orders: Amoxil Suspension 500mg every 12 hours for seven days by mouth	
Instructions: Notify HCP if Tanisha continues to complain of mouth soreness after 72 hours.	
Follow-up visit: Feb. 16, yr	**Lab work or Tests:** None
Signature: *Dr. Chen Lee*	**Date:** Feb. 2, yr

Posted by: Date: Time: Verified by: Date: Time:

1. Circle the new medication order.
2. What is the dose ordered?   _____
3. What is the frequency ordered?   _____
4. Place a checkmark next to Tanisha's current medications
5. Does Tanisha have any medication allergies? _____

Massachusetts | Responsibilities in Action   54

People Who Manage Appointments Independently

When a person manages their medical appointments independently your responsibilities will vary depending on the person. Your responsibilities may include:

- Reminding the person of the upcoming appointment date and time
- Ensuring the person has all necessary documents, such as a HCP order form
- Reviewing with the person what needs to be discussed at the appointment
- Arranging transportation
- Reminding the person to obtain prescription refills

If the person does not bring back new valid orders and prescriptions, it is your responsibility to obtain them.

If going to the Emergency Room and/or Hospital

- Take the person's
  - current medication list
  - insurance card
  - HCP Encounter/Consult/Order form
- Be prepared to tell Emergency Room (ER) and/or hospital staff why you are bringing the person to the ER and/or hospital.
  - Discuss with the HCP any scheduled medication the person may miss as a result of the ER and/or hospital visit.
- If you have any concerns about taking the person home (or to work/day program) after the visit, tell the ER and/or hospital staff and contact your supervisor before leaving the hospital.

After a hospital admission, before the person is discharged back to the program, medication reconciliation is required. Medication reconciliation is comparing the hospital discharge orders to the orders prior to admission; any discrepancies must be clarified with the HCP. An ER visit is not considered a hospital admission.

Medication reconciliation ensures new medication ordered during a hospital stay is not omitted when the person returns home. It also ensures medication that was discontinued during a hospital stay is not administered when the person returns home.

Massachusetts | Responsibilities in Action

Medication Reconciliation/Discharge Orders (Sample Guide)

Medication reconciliation is the process of generating the most complete and accurate list of the individual's currently prescribed medication. This must be done during every transition of care (e.g., transferred to/from a health-care facility, hospital, nursing home, crisis stabilization unit or rehabilitation center, etc.).

Discharge (new) orders from the Health Care facility supersede (take the place of) prior existing orders. Any discrepancies identified must be immediately brought to the attention of the prescribing Health Care Provider (HCP). Document that the prescribing HCP has been informed.

Checklist

1. Before the individual is discharged from the Health Care Facility:

    ☐ Obtain all HCP orders that were in place prior to the admission (from the individual's home).

    ☐ Obtain the new HCP medication orders being prescribed (using the Health Care Facility discharge orders.)

    ☐ Compare the medication on the two sets of HCP orders (new and prior); bear in mind the 5 rights. Pay particular attention to dose and/or frequency changes for medications that appear on both sets of orders.

    ☐ If there are discrepancies between the two sets of orders; review these with the HCP prior to discharge.

    ☐ Be sure to obtain signed, dated, HCP orders. If there is more than one page of HCP orders, each page must be signed and dated by the HCP. An image of the provider's signature is acceptable. Electronic Health Care Provider signatures are acceptable. An electronic signature is a signature from a system that complies with 105 CMR 721.000 Standards for Prescription Format and Security in Massachusetts. Only the last page of the HCP orders needs to be (electronically) signed and dated by the HCP.

    ☐ Obtain any new prescriptions or ensure that the correct pharmacy has been notified by the HCP of any new medication prescriptions.

2. Once the individual has returned home:

    ☐ Notify the Primary Care Physician (PCP), and any other prescribing HCP, that the individual had a transfer of care.

    ☐ Notify the PCP, and any other prescribing HCP, of any new or changed medication/treatment orders or previously ordered medications omitted from the Health Care Facility discharge orders.

    ☐ Obtain from the PCP and any other prescribing HCP, orders for any previously scheduled medications/treatments that they want reordered (and are not on the new Health Care Facility discharge orders).

    ☐ Obtain any newly prescribed medication from the pharmacy.

    ☐ Transcribe, Post, and Verify Health Care Facility discharge orders and newly reordered medications.

    ☐ Communicate the changes to other involved in supporting the individual (e.g., coworkers, supervisor, day program staff, family members, etc.) according to agency policy.

Fax Health Care Provider Orders

It is preferred that fax orders be used in place of telephone orders. A fax order is a legal order. Ask the HCP to fax you a copy of the order (if your agency's confidentiality policy permits this) to save time and help prevent errors. To protect the person's confidentiality, wait at the fax machine for the transmission.

Telephone Health Care Provider Orders

HCP orders by telephone are allowed. A telephone order is documentation of instructions given by a HCP over the telephone. The instructions may include a newly ordered medication, a change to an existing medication order, or a non-medication order such as, to begin monitoring a person's weight every week.

Telephone orders are sometimes necessary. For example, blood work results become available 3 hours after the HCP appointment. Based on those results the HCP determines a new medication or a medication change is needed and calls to give you a telephone order for the new medication.

When you take a telephone order:

- Document the order word-for-word on a HCP Telephone Order form
- Read back the information given to you by the HCP to confirm you recorded it accurately
- If you're having trouble understanding the HCP, ask another staff to listen in as you take the order
  - then have that staff read it back and sign the order too
- If you do not know how to spell a spoken word, ask the HCP to spell it
- Draw lines through any blank spaces in the order
- To help ensure accuracy, if you are the staff that obtains the telephone order, you should be the staff to transcribe the order
- Make sure the HCP signs the original order within 72 hours
  - Staff may administer a medication while waiting for the signature for the first 72 hours

Provide the pharmacy contact information to the HCP you are speaking to, so the HCP will send a prescription that corresponds with the telephone order. Call the pharmacy to see if the prescription was received and when the medication will be ready for pick up or when it will be delivered.

Telephone orders are posted and verified twice:
- First when the order is initially obtained
- Again after the HCP has signed the order, ensuring there were no changes

Although MAP allows Certified staff to take a telephone order, some providers do not. Ask your supervisor if the provider you work for allows you to take a telephone order, if so, ask where the telephone order forms are kept at your work location.

Sample HCP Telephone/Fax Order Form

Program address: Telephone/Fax:

Date of telephone/fax order: Time of telephone/fax order:

Name of person: Allergies:

Discontinue:

New order:

Generic Name:

Brand Name:

Dose:

Frequency:

Route:

Reason for Medication/Change:

Special Instructions/Precautions (include instructions for common side effects):

If in a self-administering training program, include number of days person may package and hold:

If vital signs are required, list guidelines:

Date of next lab work (if any):

HCP Name (print):

HCP telephone number:

HCP fax number:

Staff Signature/Title: Date:

Posted by: Date: Time:

Verified by: Date: Time:

HCP Signature: Date:

Posted by: Date: Time:

Verified by: Date: Time:

Massachusetts | Responsibilities in Action

Answer the following HCP Telephone Order questions.

1. Are MAP Certified staff allowed to take a telephone order? _____

2. What must you do to ensure you have taken the telephone order correctly?
   _____
   _____

3. A telephone order must be signed by the HCP within how many hours? _____

4. May this medication be administered before the HCP signs the order? _____

Exhausting a Current Supply of Medication

If there is a new order to change the dose or frequency of a medication a person is currently on, it is acceptable to exhaust (use) the current supply of medication until the new prescription is filled.

You must verify with the pharmacist that the supply of medication on hand may be used according to the new prescription directions.

In addition, the following must be in place:

- A new HCP order reflecting the change
  - The medication block for the old order will be marked as discontinued on the medication sheet
  - The new order is transcribed on to a medication sheet
- The medication strength on hand allows for safe preparation
  - Examples:
    - A 10mg dose is increased to a 20mg dose
    - A frequency is changed from morning to night
- The medication container has a 'directions change' sticker
  - A brightly colored sticker may be used in place of a directions change sticker
    - The sticker is placed close to but does not cover the pharmacy label directions
  - A directions change sticker may only be used for a maximum of 30 days

Note the directions change sticker is placed close to but does not cover the original pharmacy label directions.

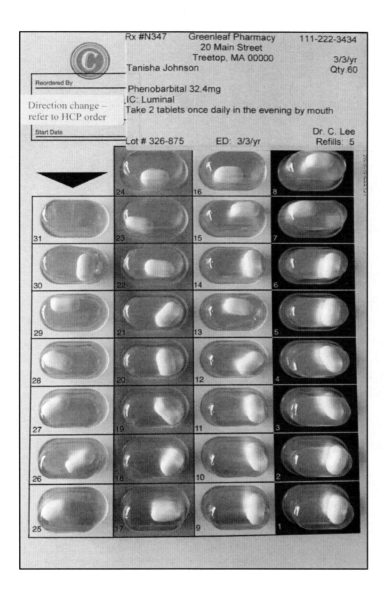

If you see a 'directions change' or brightly colored sticker on a medication container, you will know there is a new HCP order. This means the information between the new HCP order and the information on the old pharmacy label will not agree until a new label is applied by the pharmacy.

Within 30 days of receiving the new HCP order, the pharmacy label must reflect the new HCP order.

HEALTH CARE PROVIDER ORDER

Name: Tanisha Johnson	**Date:** March 18, yr
Health Care Provider: Dr. Lee	**Allergies:** No Known Allergies
Reason for Visit: Tanisha has had a recent increase in seizure activity. See seizure data.	
Current Medications: Clonazepam 1mg twice daily, at 8am and 4pm by mouth Phenobarbital 64.8mg once daily in the evening by mouth	
Staff Signature: *Sam Dowd*	**Date:** March 18, yr
Health Care Provider Findings: Seizure data reviewed reflects an increase in seizure activity.	
Medication/Treatment Orders: DC Phenobarbital 64.8mg once daily in the evening by mouth Phenobarbital 97.2mg once daily in the evening by mouth	
Instructions:	
Follow-up visit: 3 months	**Lab work or Tests:** Phenobarbital level
Signature: *Dr. Chen Lee*	**Date:** March 18, yr

Posted: **Sam Dowd** Date: 3/18/yr Time: 2pm Verified: Linda White Date: 3/18/yr Time: 4pm

Note the medication supply being exhausted on the previous page. Review the new HCP order above to answer the question below.

You will no longer administer 2 tablets once daily in the evening according to the directions on the pharmacy label. How many tablets will you now administer once daily in the evening? _____

Massachusetts | Responsibilities in Action

Let's Review

- Preparation before a HCP visit will help to ensure a successful appointment
- During a HCP appointment make sure
    - The person participates in the appointment and/or you advocate, as needed
    - You obtain new HCP orders that
        - include the 5 rights of medication administration
        - are signed and dated by the HCP
            - electronic HCP signatures are acceptable
        - agree with prescriptions
            - if a prescription is obtained
    - the HCP sent new prescriptions or prescription refill requests to the correct pharmacy
        - After the appointment ensure medications are obtained from the pharmacy
- If a person attends a HCP visit without your help and does not bring back new valid orders and prescriptions, it is your responsibility to obtain them
- Prescriptions may not be used in place of a HCP order
- Changes are communicated to all staff involved in the person's care
- Basic information needed for an emergency room visit or hospital admission
    - reason for visit
    - current medication list
    - insurance card
    - HCP Encounter/Consult/Order form
- Medication reconciliation before a hospital discharge is required
    - Must be completed before the person leaves the hospital
- Fax orders are preferred instead of telephone orders
    - Telephone orders
        - must be posted and verified twice
        - may be administered without the HCP signature for 72 hours
        - must be signed by the HCP within 72 hours
- A current supply of medication may be exhausted if there is a dose and/or a frequency change and the strength of the tablet allows for safe preparation
- If you see a 'directions change' or brightly colored sticker on a medication container, you will know there is a new HCP order and you cannot rely on the directions printed on the pharmacy label.

Unit 5

Obtaining, Storing and Securing Medication

Responsibilities you will learn

- The difference between a HCP order and a prescription
- What you do if the medication looks different from the last time it was obtained
- Where the medication storage keys are kept when in use and when not in use
- How to access the backup set of medication keys

Obtaining Medication

A current HCP order is required to administer medications and dietary supplements to people living at MAP registered programs. If there is no HCP order you may not administer the medication.

A HCP order is a set of instructions, from the HCP to the staff at the program, instructing the staff what medication the person is to receive and how it is to be administered.

A prescription must be provided by the HCP for every medication ordered; this includes controlled, countable controlled, OTC medications and dietary supplements. A prescription is a set of instructions, from the HCP to the pharmacist, instructing the pharmacist what medication to prepare and how it is to be administered to the person. The pharmacist uses the information on the prescription to print a pharmacy label.

There are many ways the HCP can provide the prescription to the pharmacy, such as:

- Electronic
- Telephone
- A paper prescription can be handed to you or the person it is written for (if self-administering), to bring to the pharmacy.

Typically, the HCP will write the brand name of the medication on the order and the prescription. The pharmacy will supply the generic form of the medication.
To ensure that the HCP order and pharmacy label agree, if the pharmacy supplies the generic form of the medication, the label must also include the brand name.

If the HCP orders the generic form of the medication only the generic name needs to be on the pharmacy label.

Review the HCP order and note the brand name medication that is circled. The generic medication is substituted by the pharmacy. The corresponding pharmacy label on the next page has both the generic and brand names circled.

HEALTH CARE PROVIDER ORDER

Name: David Cook	**Date:** June 1, yr
Health Care Provider: Dr. Black	**Allergies:** No Known Allergies
Reason for Visit: David states that he has burning in his throat after eating.	
Current Medications: Zestril 40 mg by mouth once a day in the morning. Check blood pressure before administering medication. If systolic reading is less than 100, hold medication and notify HCP. Motrin 400 mg by mouth as needed every 8 hours for right knee pain. Notify HCP if right knee pain continues for more than 48 hours.	
Staff Signature: **Sam Dowd**	**Date:** June 1, yr
Health Care Provider Findings: Gastroesophageal reflux disease (GERD)	
Medication/Treatment Orders: Prilosec 20 mg by mouth once a day before supper	
Instructions: remain upright 30 minutes after eating	
Follow-up visit: 1 month	**Lab work or Tests:** None today
Signature: *Richard Black, MD*	**Date:** June 1, yr

Posted by: Date: Time: **Verified by:**   Date: Time:

Massachusetts | Responsibilities in Action

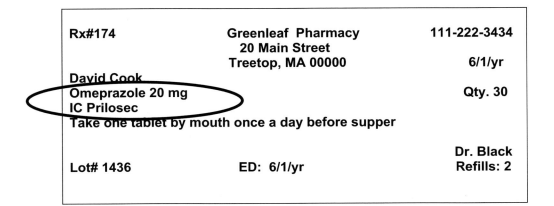

Once the HCP orders a medication, the expectation is, the person will receive the medication as ordered. There must be a system in place to ensure the medication is obtained from the pharmacy in a timely manner.

For example:

- You must contact the pharmacy to ensure the prescription was received. Once the medication has been prepared by the pharmacy, you must
    - pick up the medication at the pharmacy or
    - confirm a date and time that the pharmacy will deliver the medication to the program

Every program must have a method for obtaining medication from the pharmacy.
For example:

- You pick up new or refilled medication from the pharmacy
- The pharmacy delivers new or refilled medication to the home
- The pharmacy supplies automatic refills

If medication is delivered to the program while you are busy, you should ask the driver to wait until you can accept the delivery, verify the contents against the ordering and receiving log and sign for the medication.

Ask your Supervisor what method is used to obtain medication refills from the pharmacy at your work location.

Massachusetts | Responsibilities in Action

If a new medication is ordered by the HCP and there is a delay in obtaining the medication from the pharmacy for any reason, such as when prior authorization is needed from an insurance company, if guardian consent is required or if an antipsychotic medication prescribed requires court approval under a Rogers Decision; you must contact the HCP immediately and obtain orders stating what should be done until the medication is obtained.

If a new medication is ordered and the pharmacy service typically used by your work location is not available, ask your Supervisor which alternative pharmacy is to be used instead to obtain the medication.

Antipsychotic medications are used to decrease symptoms of mental illness. These medications cause side effects.

In November 1983, the Massachusetts Supreme Judicial Court issued a decision that is called the 'Rogers Decision'. This gave persons who take antipsychotic medications new rights. These rights help protect them from the overuse of these medications and are limited to a required maximum daily dose that a HCP can order.

Ask your Supervisor if there are HCP orders for antipsychotic medications requiring a Rogers Decision at your work location.

Pharmacy Label Components

Medication received from the pharmacy may be packaged in a plastic container, bottle or tamper resistant package, such as a blister pack. Whatever the packaging, it must be labeled by the pharmacy.

The pharmacy label typically contains the following information:

1. Prescription Rx number (Rx is an abbreviation for medical prescriptions. It is used to obtain refills.)
2. Pharmacy name
3. Pharmacy telephone number (It is used to contact the pharmacy or a pharmacist.)
4. Name of the person
5. Date the medication was dispensed
6. Name of the medication
    a. Generic
    b. Brand
7. Strength of medication supplied (how much medication is in each tablet, capsule or mL supplied)
8. Total amount of medication dispensed (# of tablets, capsules or mL in the container)
9. Amount of tablets, capsules or mL to be administered
10. Route to administer the medication
11. Frequency to administer the medication
12. Special instructions
13. The HCP's name
14. Lot number (A number that is assigned to each batch of medication produced. All medication from the same batch shares the same lot number.)
15. Expiration date (the last date the medication may be administered). Typically, the words, expiration date are abbreviated on a label as ED or Exp. Examples of other words that may be printed on a pharmacy label instead of 'expiration date', include but are not limited to, 'Discard After' or 'Use By' followed by the date.
16. Number of refills (how many remaining times the medication may be obtained from the pharmacy)

Number the pharmacy label items below with the corresponding numbered (1-16) pharmacy label components listed on the previous page.

☐ Rx # C201   ☐ Greenleaf Pharmacy   ☐ 111-222-3434
                    20 Main Street
                    Treetop, MA 00000   ☐ 3/4/yr

☐ David Cook

☐ Tramadol ☐ 50mg

☐ IC Ultram
                                           ☐ Qty. 21
Take ☐ 1 tablet ☐ by mouth ☐ every 8 hours for 7 days
   ☐ Take with water
                                           ☐ Dr. Black
   ☐ Lot # 776-5433   ☐ ED: 3/4/yr   ☐ Refills: 0

Often you learn about medication recalls on the news, if you do, contact the pharmacy with the medication name and follow the pharmacists' recommendations.

Massachusetts | Responsibilities in Action

Answer the following questions by choosing the best response.

1. The expiration date on a pharmacy label is the

    A. ___ Date the pharmacy last filled the prescription
    B. ___ Date the prescription was purchased at the pharmacy
    C. ___ Last date the medication may be administered
    D. ___ Last date to call in a refill

2. The Rx # (number) is used to obtain a

    A. ___ New HCP order
    B. ___ Renewal of the prescription
    C. ___ Medication refill
    D. ___ Newly prescribed medication

3. There is a 7 day supply of medication available for a person; you need what information to refill this medication before it runs out?

    A. ___ Lot #
    B. ___ Generic name
    C. ___ Expiration date
    D. ___ Rx #

4. The pharmacy phone number can be used for many reasons. Check all that apply:

    A. ___ Determine when a medication will be delivered to the program
    B. ___ Call in refills
    C. ___ Determine when a medication will be available for pick up
    D. ___ Ask about possible medication interactions and/or side effects
    E. ___ Ask if the strength of tablet on hand may be used with a change in a medication order

Remember, it is your responsibility to learn about a medication before you administer it. The pharmacist and the medication information sheet are both excellent resources for medication information.

Ensuring the Pharmacy Provides the Correct Medication

One of your most important responsibilities is to ensure the pharmacy has supplied the medication as ordered by the HCP. As soon as the medication is obtained, compare the pharmacy label to the HCP order; both must agree.

Look at the medication. At times, the pharmacy will purchase the same medication from different pharmaceutical companies; depending on the pharmaceutical company used, the same medication might look different. If the medication is different in color, shape, size or markings from the last time it was filled you must contact the MAP Consultant before administering it.

If the strength of the tablet supplied by the pharmacy will not allow the correct dose to be administered you must return the medication to the pharmacy to obtain the correct strength. For example, the dose ordered is 75mg and the pharmacy provides 50 mg tablets.

Some pharmacy labels include a description of the medication on the container. If included, read the description of the medication and compare it to the medication in the container.

Also, you must check the strength of tablet supplied; it may have changed from the last time the medication was obtained.

A person has a HCP order for Topiramate 100mg twice daily. The pharmacy had been supplying Topiramate 25mg tablet (round and white) with instructions to give 4 tablets twice daily. When the following month's refill was obtained, the pharmacy supplied Topiramate 100mg tablet (round and pink), with instructions to give 1 tablet twice daily.

1. What could happen if you did not read the label closely to see the strength and amount had changed? _____
2. In addition to the label directions changing, what is different about the appearance of the tablet? _____

When the pharmacy label directions change, for example, a different strength tablet was supplied; the current transcription on the medication sheet must be marked through to indicate that the transcription was rewritten to reflect the pharmacy label changes. See example below:

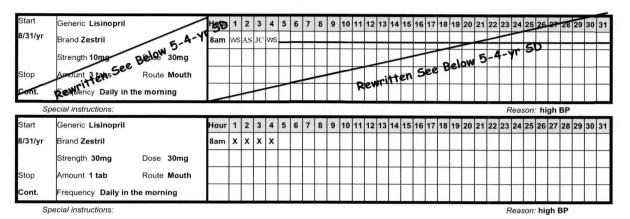

When to Request a Medication Refill

A medication refill should be requested when there is no less than a seven-day supply of medication remaining. This is to ensure medication is available to administer as ordered.

To determine when there is no less than a seven-day supply of medication remaining, you must review the dose and frequency in the HCP order. In addition, you must review the pharmacy label to know the strength of the tablet supplied and the total amount of tablets needed to administer daily.

If the ordered refill does not arrive with the pharmacy delivery, make sure you immediately contact the pharmacy to determine when the medication will be obtained.

When the last refill is obtained, immediately contact the person's HCP and request a new prescription be submitted to the pharmacy. Contacting the HCP immediately will allow 30 days for the HCP to send a prescription to the pharmacy.

Class Discussion

Juanita Gomez has a HCP order for Phenytoin 200mg twice daily by mouth. The pharmacy supplies the medication in 100mg strength capsules. Look at the medication package and answer the following questions.

1. How many capsules are needed for a 30-day supply? _____
2. How many capsules are currently in the package? _____
3. How many capsules would you expect to see if there was a 7-day supply left in the package? _____
4. Is it time to request a refill? _____
5. Why or why not? _____
6. How many capsules should there be in the package when you request a refill? __
7. Why is it important to order a refill when a 7-day supply remains instead of a 3-day supply? _____

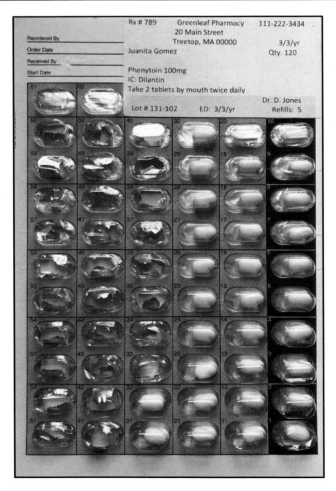

Tracking Medication

After medication has been obtained from the pharmacy it must be documented as received into the program and tracked. All programs must maintain a record of when a prescription is filled and the quantity of medication dispensed by the pharmacy; this is documented using a Medication Ordering and Receiving Log. Medications are also documented and tracked using:

- Pharmacy receipts
- Count Book
- Medication sheets
- Medication release documents such as
  - Leave of Absence (LOA) form
    - when medication is administered away from a program
  - Transfer Form
    - when medication is moved from one location to another
- Disposal records

Medication Storage and Security

The following are medication storage requirements, including liquid and refrigerated medication:

- All medication is key locked
- Countable medication must be
    - Double key locked
        - a key lock within a key lock
    - packaged in tamper resistant packaging
    - liquid countable medication must be packaged so that once used, the container is empty; you may not use a multi-dose bottle of a liquid countable medication
        - Some liquid countable medication is packaged by the manufacturer in the specific dose ordered; if not
            - the pharmacy must prepare a single dose of liquid countable medication into an oral dosing syringe and close with a tamper resistant seal.

- Only items required for medication administration may be stored in the locked medication area
- Medication must remain in the original, labeled, packaging received from the pharmacy
- When a medication supply is running low; do not mix the supply of medication in the current bottle with the new supply of medication, even if it is the same medication and strength. Each medication should remain in its originally dispensed container.
- Each person must have their own medication storage container with their name
- Medication taken by mouth must be separated from medication taken by other routes; this will help decrease the possibility of a medication being administered by the wrong route
- The medication storage/preparation area should have minimal distractions; this will help you to remain mindful while preparing medication for administration
    - Avoid distractions from other people
    - Turn off your cell phone

- Store medication away from
  - food and/or toxic substances such as household cleaners
  - excessive heat, moisture and/or light; these factors can result in the medication becoming less effective

Ask your Supervisor where medications requiring refrigeration are stored at your work location.

You must carry the medication storage keys if you are assigned medication administration duties for the shift.

There must also be a backup set of keys accessed through contact with administrative staff in the event there is an issue with the first set. (Administrative staff is someone who typically does not work in the program.)

For example:

- There are two combination locked boxes located in the program
  - Each 'box' contains a set of medication keys
- The combination to the 1st box is known only to MAP Certified staff in the program
- The combination to the 2nd box is known only to administrative staff
- In the event there is an issue with the 1st set of keys
  - MAP Certified staff calls the administrative staff for the combination
  - The combination must be changed afterwards by administrative staff

Ask your Supervisor how you access the backup set of keys at your work location, if needed.

Massachusetts | Responsibilities in Action

Let's Review

- A HCP order is required to administer all medication and dietary supplements
- The HCP must provide a prescription for each medication and/or dietary supplement ordered
- The pharmacist uses the prescription to prepare and label medication
- Medication must remain in the packaging received from the pharmacy
- You must compare what is received from the pharmacy ensuring it agrees with what the HCP ordered
- When medication is received from the pharmacy, you must check the color, shape, size and/or markings of the medication; if different from the last time it was obtained, a MAP Consultant must be contacted
- Check to see if the strength of the tablet received changed from the last refill
- Request medication refills when there is no less than a seven-day supply left
- All medications must be key locked
- All countable medications must be
    - double key locked
    - in tamper resistant packaging
    - tracked
    - counted
- Medication storage keys must remain on the person assigned medication administration duties for the shift
- Backup keys are accessed only through contact with administrative staff

Unit 6

Recording Information

Responsibilities you will learn

- The purpose of a medication sheet
- How to transcribe information from a HCP order and pharmacy label onto a medication sheet
- Acceptable abbreviations for use on a medication sheet
- How to 'Post and Verify' a HCP order

To **transcribe** is to copy information from one document and record it onto another document, the completed document is a **transcription**. When a HCP order is written and medication is obtained from the pharmacy, the information from the HCP order and pharmacy label must be transcribed (copied) onto a medication sheet.

HEALTH CARE PROVIDER ORDER

Name: David Cook	**Date:** March 3, yr
Health Care Provider: Dr. Black	**Allergies:** No Known Allergies
Reason for Visit: David states his 'head hurts' and he has had a runny nose for 2 days, temperature is 100.3	
Current Medications: Amoxil 500mg three times daily for 10 days by mouth Also, see attached medication list.	
Staff Signature: *Kay Mathers*	**Date:** March 3, yr
Health Care Provider Findings: Sinus infection	
Medication/Treatment Orders: DC Amoxil EES 666mg three times daily for 10 days by mouth	
Instructions: Call HCP if temperature remains elevated above 100.3 for more than 48 hours	
Follow-up visit:	**Lab work or Tests:** None today
Signature: Richard Black, MD	**Date:** March 3, yr

Posted by: Date: Time: **Verified by: Date: Time:**

Pharmacy Label

Rx # 156	**Greenleaf Pharmacy** **20 Main Street** **Treetop, MA 09111**	**111-222-3434** **3/3/yr**
David Cook **Erythromycin 333mg** **IC EES** **Take 2 tablets by mouth three times daily for 10 days**		**Qty.60**
		Dr. Black
Lot # 14239	**ED: 3/3/yr**	**Refills: 0**

Month and Year: **MEDICATION ADMINISTRATION SHEET**   **Allergies:**

Start	Generic		Hour	1	2	3	4	5	6	7	8	9	10	11	12	13	14	15	16	17	18	19	20	21	22	23	24	25	26	27	28	29	30	31
	Brand																																	
	Strength	Dose																																
Stop	Amount	Route																																
	Frequency																																	

Special instructions: Reason:

Start	Generic		Hour	1	2	3	4	5	6	7	8	9	10	11	12	13	14	15	16	17	18	19	20	21	22	23	24	25	26	27	28	29	30	31
	Brand																																	
	Strength	Dose																																
Stop	Amount	Route																																
	Frequency																																	

Special instructions: Reason:

Start	Generic		Hour	1	2	3	4	5	6	7	8	9	10	11	12	13	14	15	16	17	18	19	20	21	22	23	24	25	26	27	28	29	30	31
	Brand																																	
	Strength	Dose																																
Stop	Amount	Route																																
	Frequency																																	

Special instructions: Reason:

Start	Generic		Hour	1	2	3	4	5	6	7	8	9	10	11	12	13	14	15	16	17	18	19	20	21	22	23	24	25	26	27	28	29	30	31
	Brand																																	
	Strength	Dose																																
Stop	Amount	Route																																
	Frequency																																	

Special instructions: Reason:

	CODES			Signature			Signature	
Name:	DP-day program/day hab							
	LOA-leave of absence							
Site:	P-packaged							
	W-work							
	H-hospital, nursing home, rehab center							
	S-school							

Accuracy Check 1 _____ Date _____ Time _____   Accuracy Check 2 _____ Date _____ Time _____

To transcribe a new medication order, you will be using the HCP order, the pharmacy label and the medication sheet.

Massachusetts | Responsibilities in Action   80

2020 The Massachusetts Departments of Public Health, Developmental Services, Mental Health, Children and Families and the Rehabilitation Commission

Abbreviations

An abbreviation is a shortened form of a word or phrase. There are many abbreviations used in the health care profession however there are only a few abbreviations you are allowed to use in a MAP program. When transcribing onto a medication sheet, the following abbreviations are acceptable for use:

- Cont.- continue
- DC - discontinue
- am - morning
- pm - afternoon or evening
- cap - capsule
- tab - tablet
- gm - gram
- mg - milligram
- mcg - microgram
- IU or units - international unit
- mL - milliliter
- PRN - as needed
- IM - intramuscular
- ODT - orally dissolving tablet
- Subcut - subcutaneous

True (T) or False (F)

1. ___ Only acceptable abbreviations may be used on the medication sheet
2. ___ Each program may create their own list of acceptable abbreviations
3. ___ The abbreviation pm can indicate either afternoon or evening
4. ___ The abbreviation for milligram is mL
5. ___ PRN is the abbreviation for as needed

The Medication Record

A medication record typically contains:

- Emergency Fact Sheet (EFS)
- HCP Orders
- Medication Sheets
- Medication Information Sheets

Medication Sheet

All HCP medication orders must be transcribed onto a medication sheet. The medication sheet is a document that tracks the administration of medications for each person who has medication ordered. This is typically done on a monthly basis.

Each time you administer a medication, you will sign your initials on the medication sheet, documenting you have administered the medication as ordered. At the end of each month, the completed medication sheets are removed from the medication book and the new month's medication sheets are inserted; the past month's medication sheets are kept and filed.

Other terms used for a medication sheet include: med sheet, medication administration sheet, medication administration record (MAR) and/or medication log.

Month and Year	MEDICATION ADMINISTRATION SHEET	Allergies:

Start	Generic		Hour	1	2	3	4	5	6	7	8	9	10	11	12	13	14	15	16	17	18	19	20	21	22	23	24	25	26	27	28	29	30	31
	Brand																																	
	Strength	Dose																																
Stop	Amount	Route																																
	Frequency																																	

Special instructions: *Reason:*

Start	Generic		Hour	1	2	3	4	5	6	7	8	9	10	11	12	13	14	15	16	17	18	19	20	21	22	23	24	25	26	27	28	29	30	31
	Brand																																	
	Strength	Dose																																
Stop	Amount	Route																																
	Frequency																																	

Special instructions: *Reason:*

Start	Generic		Hour	1	2	3	4	5	6	7	8	9	10	11	12	13	14	15	16	17	18	19	20	21	22	23	24	25	26	27	28	29	30	31
	Brand																																	
	Strength	Dose																																
Stop	Amount	Route																																
	Frequency																																	

Special instructions: *Reason:*

Start	Generic		Hour	1	2	3	4	5	6	7	8	9	10	11	12	13	14	15	16	17	18	19	20	21	22	23	24	25	26	27	28	29	30	31
	Brand																																	
	Strength	Dose																																
Stop	Amount	Route																																
	Frequency																																	

Special instructions: *Reason:*

	CODES		Signature		Signature
Name:	DP-day program/day hab				
	LOA-leave of absence				
Site:	P-packaged				
	W-work				
	H-hospital, nursing home, rehab center				
	S-school				

Accuracy Check 1 _____ Date _____ Time _____   Accuracy Check 2 _____ Date _____ Time _____

2020 The Massachusetts Departments of Public Health, Developmental Services, Mental Health, Children and Families and the Rehabilitation Commission

A Detailed View of the Medication Sheet

The top of the medication sheet includes the:
- current month and year and
- allergies

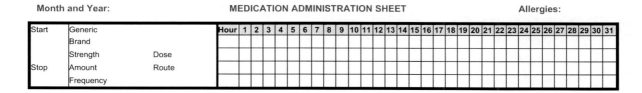

The left side (medication block) of the medication sheet has an area to write:

- Generic and brand medication names
- Strength of the medication
- Amount of medication to administer
- Frequency or how often the medication is to be administered
- Dose of the medication
- Route by which the medication is to be administered
- Start date
- Stop date

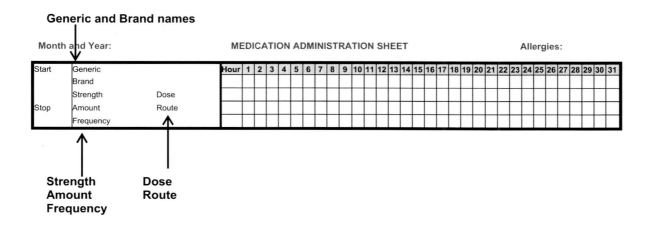

Start Date and Stop Date

A start date is the date the person receives the first dose of a medication. Start dates are used to monitor how long a person has been receiving a medication without any changes to the HCP order. If a person has been receiving a medication for a long time, without the HCP order changing, the start date may be several years old.

A stop date is used to identify the date when:
- The last dose of a time limited medication is administered; such as an antibiotic that is administered for only 7 days or
- If the medication is not time limited and will be given on an ongoing basis, the stop date is documented as 'cont.' (continue).

Start date

Month and Year: ⬇ MEDICATION ADMINISTRATION SHEET Allergies:

Start	Generic		Hour	1	2	3	4	5	6	7	8	9	10	11	12	13	14	15	16	17	18	19	20	21	22	23	24	25	26	27	28	29	30	31
	Brand																																
	Strength	Dose																															
Stop	Amount	Route																															
⬆	Frequency																																

Stop date

Medication Grid

The right side of the medication sheet is called the 'grid'; each box in the grid is a 'medication box'. The medication box is where you will document your initials after administering a medication. Your initials in a medication box means you have prepared and administered the medication as ordered.

Across the top of the grid are the numbers 1-31; these are the days of the month. Specific times will be written in the hour column to indicate when the medication is to be administered.

The reason for the medication (as noted in the HCP order) and/or any special instructions, are written under the medication grid.

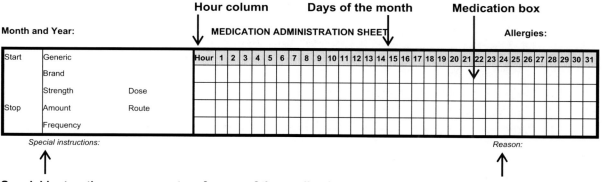

The reason a medication is ordered must be obtained from and documented by the prescribing HCP. As long as the reason does not change, historical HCP documentation stating the reason for the medication is acceptable and may be filed in the person's health record.

The bottom of the medication sheet includes the:
- Person's name
- Address
- List of acceptable 'codes' for use on the medication sheet
- Signature list
    - Each staff must initial and sign the signature list as a way to identify their initials with their full name anytime initials are used on a medication sheet. For example, you will initial and sign the signature list once for the month the first time you administer medication or if you make any changes to the medication sheet, such as when discontinuing a medication.
- Accuracy Checks
    - Prior to the first medication administration of the new month, 2 staff preferably together, check the new month's medication sheets for accuracy using the HCP orders and pharmacy labels ensuring that the orders were transcribed onto the new month's medication sheets.
        - Also review the current month's medication sheets to ensure all ongoing transcriptions were copied onto the new medication sheets.
    - Documentation of a completed accuracy check includes your full signature, the date and the time completed.
        - Accuracy check documentation at the bottom of the new medication sheet(s) indicates that they are complete and correct.

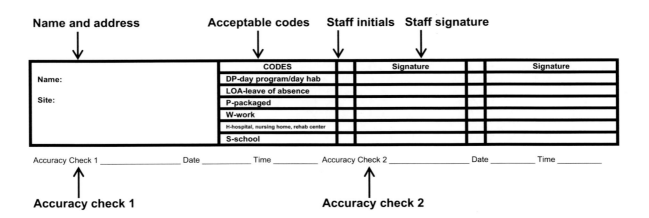

If accuracy checks have been completed several days prior to the start of the new month, staff must double check before the first medication administration of new month to ensure no changes occurred.

Acceptable Codes on a Medication Sheet

A code is a set of letters created as an acceptable abbreviation of a longer phrase or sentence that describes a specific medication responsibility, a change in medication responsibility and/or the responsibility for the medication administration to be done away from the person's home.

- A - **a**bsent from site (Medication was not administered due to unauthorized reasons beyond staff's control as the person left the program without agreement or supervision or did not return as planned without agreement or supervision during medication administration time.)
- DP - **d**ay **p**rogram/day habilitation (Person's medication responsibilities transferred to a day program or a day habilitation program)
- H - **h**ospital, nursing home, rehab center, respite (Person's medication responsibilities transferred to a hospital, nursing home, rehabilitation center, respite, etc.)
- LOA - **l**eave **o**f **a**bsence (Medication was transferred to family/guardian/responsible party for administration while on leave of absence)
- NSS - **n**o **s**econd **s**taff (Specific to medication that requires dose verification prior to administration by a second staff such as, warfarin sodium, indicates there is no second staff available.)
- OSA - **o**ff-**s**ite **a**dministration (Medication is administered by Certified staff at an off-site location, such as the movies, a community outing, etc.)
- P - **p**ackaged (Person packed their medication under staff supervision. Code is used when a person is learning to self-administer their medication)
- S - **s**chool (Person's medication responsibilities transferred to a school or after school program)
- V - **v**acation (Medication to be administered by Certified staff when the staff accompanies a person on a planned vacation)
- W - **w**ork (Medication to be administered by Certified staff at a person's work location)

Only acceptable codes may be used on the medication sheet to identify when a medication is administered

- at a location other than the person's home or
- if the person is learning to self-administer their medication or
- if the person was not present during the medication administration time.

If you use an acceptable code on a medication sheet, the code and its meaning must be listed on that medication sheet.

Recorded Information on a Medication Sheet: Transcription

Before you are able to administer a medication, the information from the HCP order and the pharmacy label must be transcribed onto the medication sheet.

The following information must be transcribed onto the medication sheet:

1. The month and year
2. The person's name
3. Any known allergies or if none, write 'none' or 'no known allergies'
4. Generic medication name
5. Brand medication name
6. Dose of the medication (copied from the HCP order)
7. Strength of the medication (copied from the pharmacy label)
8. Amount to be administered (copied from the pharmacy label)
9. Frequency the medication is to be administered
10. Route the medication is to be administered
11. Start date
12. Stop date
13. Any special instructions or parameters for use
14. Reason for the medication

The allergy information on a medication sheet must be completed. Whether or not a person has allergies, the allergy section on the medication sheet must be completed so that HCPs and other staff will know this section was not overlooked.

Massachusetts | Responsibilities in Action

Write the number on the medication sheet of the term on the previous page that corresponds with information to be transcribed, listed as numbers 1-14.

MEDICATION ADMINISTRATION SHEET

Month and Year: _____   Allergies: _____

Start	Generic		Hour	1	2	3	4	5	6	7	8	9	10	11	12	13	14	15	16	17	18	19	20	21	22	23	24	25	26	27	28	29	30	31
	Brand																																
	Strength	Dose																															
Stop	Amount	Route																															
	Frequency																																

Special instructions: *Reason:*

Start	Generic		Hour	1	2	3	4	5	6	7	8	9	10	11	12	13	14	15	16	17	18	19	20	21	22	23	24	25	26	27	28	29	30	31
	Brand																																
	Strength	Dose																															
Stop	Amount	Route																															
	Frequency																																

Special instructions: *Reason:*

Start	Generic		Hour	1	2	3	4	5	6	7	8	9	10	11	12	13	14	15	16	17	18	19	20	21	22	23	24	25	26	27	28	29	30	31
	Brand																																
	Strength	Dose																															
Stop	Amount	Route																															
	Frequency																																

Special instructions: *Reason:*

Start	Generic		Hour	1	2	3	4	5	6	7	8	9	10	11	12	13	14	15	16	17	18	19	20	21	22	23	24	25	26	27	28	29	30	31
	Brand																																
	Strength	Dose																															
Stop	Amount	Route																															
	Frequency																																

Special instructions: *Reason:*

	CODES		Signature		Signature
Name:	DP-day program/day hab				
	LOA-leave of absence				
Site:	P-packaged				
	W-work				
	H-hospital, nursing home, rehab center				
	S-school				

Accuracy Check 1 _____ Date _____ Time _____   Accuracy Check 2 _____ Date _____ Time _____

Massachusetts | Responsibilities in Action   89

2020 The Massachusetts Departments of Public Health, Developmental Services, Mental Health, Children and Families and the Rehabilitation Commission

Depending on the pharmacy used by your work location, you may see 'pharmacy generated medication sheets'. Pharmacy generated medication sheets have all of the information from the HCP order and the pharmacy label already recorded on it by the pharmacy.

If your program uses pharmacy generated medication sheets, you are still responsible for verifying that all information is accurate by comparing the HCP order and the pharmacy label to what is printed on the pharmacy generated medication sheet.

When pharmacy generated medication sheets are utilized, if you are part way through the month and a new HCP order is written, you will need to transcribe the new HCP order onto a blank space on the pharmacy generated medication sheet and cannot rely on the pharmacy to complete the process.

Frequency

'Frequency' and the word 'time' are used interchangeably. Most HCPs will not order an actual time to administer the medication but instead will order how many times per day a medication is to be administered or the time between doses, for example:

- Twice daily
- Three times daily
- Once daily before bedtime
- Three times daily after meals
- Every 6 hours
- Every 12 hours
- PRN every 12 hours

HCP orders are written this way so that specific medication administration times may be chosen by your supervisor, based on a person's daily schedule. Times will vary from program to program or person to person. Each program must have a medication administration time schedule. In general, unless otherwise indicated by the HCP, medication dose times should be scheduled at least 4 hours apart.

Ask your supervisor what the medication administration time schedule is specific to your work location.

HCP orders for 'once daily' medications must be further clarified to include which portion of the day the medication should be administered, such as:

- Once daily in the am (morning)
- Once daily after lunch
- Once daily before bedtime
- Once daily in the pm (afternoon or evening)

This ensures 'once daily' medications are given at an appropriate time of day. For example, some medications may cause sleepiness. Administering a medication that may cause sleepiness in the evening is a safer option than administering it in the morning.

When writing times in the hour column, it is important to write the time in the appropriate hour box. It is best practice to write 'am' times in the top two boxes and 'pm' times in the bottom two boxes.

Once daily at 4pm	Twice daily	Three times daily	Four times daily	PRN every 12 hours

Hour		Hour		Hour		Hour		Hour
		8am		8am		8am		P
						12pm		R
4pm				4pm		4pm		N
		8pm		8pm		8pm		

Except for medications ordered PRN, a specific time must be written underneath the word 'Hour' in the hour column, on the medication sheet. Do not use references to time such as breakfast, lunch, dinner or bedtime.

For example:

Sally's HCP writes an order for Depakote 250 mg daily at bedtime by mouth. Sally's typical bedtime is 9 pm. When transcribing the HCP order, remember that you must assign the medication administration time. The time is documented in the hour column on the medication administration record. In this example 9 pm is documented in the hour column to indicate Sally's preferred bedtime using the bottom 'pm' hour box.

Hour
9pm

Massachusetts | Responsibilities in Action 91

1. Tim's HCP writes an order for Depakote 500 mg daily at bedtime by mouth. His typical bedtime is 10pm. Document the time chosen in the hour column using the appropriate hour box.

Hour

2. Andrew's HCP writes an order for Omeprazole 20 mg daily thirty minutes before breakfast by mouth. His typical breakfast time is 8 am. Document the time chosen in the hour column using the appropriate hour box.

Hour

Occasionally, the HCP may want a medication to be administered at a specific time, when this is the case, the HCP will order the specific time, such as:

- Once daily at 6:30pm
- Twice daily at 10am and 7pm

When the HCP order indicates a specific time, the specific time written in the HCP order is transcribed in the hour column on the medication sheet. The time the HCP has chosen must be used even if this time varies from the programs' medication administration time schedule.

1. Kevin's HCP writes an order for Aspirin 81mg daily at 4pm by mouth. Document the time in the hour column using the appropriate hour box.

2. Mary Alice's HCP writes an order for Depakote 250mg twice daily, at 8am and 8pm by mouth. Document the times in the hour column using the appropriate hour boxes.

Remember, medication ordered PRN is an exception when transcribing in the hour column.

1. Joe's HCP writes an order for Tylenol 650mg every 6 hours PRN headache by mouth. What will you document in the hour column?

Match the term(s) to the corresponding definition.

1. ___ Start Date — A. Used when a person is not home when the medication is scheduled to be given or if the person is learning to self-administer their medication

2. ___ Special Instructions — B. Placed in a medication box to indicate you have administered the medication as ordered

3. ___ Hour Column — C. The days of the month

4. ___ Numbers 1-31 — D. Why the medication was ordered

5. ___ Reason — E. The date the person is scheduled to receive the first dose of a medication

6. ___ Stop Date — F. Location of the specific time a medication is to be administered

7. ___ Staff Initials — G. Guidelines or parameters specific to administration of the medication

8. ___ Acceptable Codes — H. The date when the last dose of a time limited medication is scheduled to be administered or if given continuously listed as 'cont.'

Transcribing a New HCP Order

When transcribing a new HCP order onto the medication sheet, always start with the first order written. Complete each new order without skipping orders in the process; this will help to ensure all orders are transcribed.

David Cook has been seen by the HCP, orders have been written and medication obtained from the pharmacy; and the date is March 3rd, yr. at 1pm. Review the following demonstration of how the information from the HCP order and pharmacy label is transcribed onto medication sheet.

HEALTH CARE PROVIDER ORDER

Name: David Cook	**Date:** March 3, yr
Health Care Provider: Dr. Black	**Allergies:** No Known Allergies
Reason for Visit: David states his 'head hurts' and he has had a runny nose for 2 days, temperature is 100.3	
Current Medications: Amoxil 500mg three times daily for 10 days by mouth Also, see attached medication list.	
Staff Signature: Sam Dowd	**Date:** March 3, yr
Health Care Provider Findings: Sinus infection	
Medication/Treatment Orders: DC Amoxil EES 666mg three times daily for 10 days by mouth	
Instructions: Call HCP if temperature remains elevated above 100.3 for more than 48 hours	
Follow-up visit:	**Lab work or Tests:** None today
Signature: Richard Black, MD	**Date:** March 3, yr

Posted by: Date: Time: Verified by: Date: Time:

Massachusetts | Responsibilities in Action

The first HCP order written states, 'DC Amoxil'.

Discontinuing a Medication
Discontinuing (DC) a medication on the medication sheet is a three-step process:

1. Cross out all open boxes on the medication sheet, next to where the medication is scheduled to be given; xxxxx's or a straight line ——— may be used.

Month and Year: March, yr	MEDICATION ADMINISTRATION SHEET	Allergies: none
Start 2/28/yr	Generic **Amoxicillin** Brand **Amoxil** Strength **250mg** Dose **500mg**	
Stop 3/10/yr	Amount **2 tabs** Route **Mouth** Frequency **Three times daily**	
Special instructions: **for 10 days**		Reason: **sinus infection**

2. Draw a diagonal line through the left side, written portion, of the medication sheet and document: DC, the date and your initials.

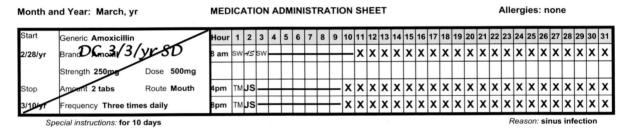

3. Draw a diagonal line through the right side, grid section, of the medication sheet and document: DC, the date and your initials.

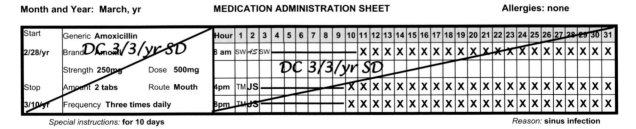

The next order you transcribe is the new medication, EES.

HEALTH CARE PROVIDER ORDER

Name: David Cook	**Date:** March 3, yr
Health Care Provider: Dr. Black	**Allergies:** No Known Allergies
Reason for Visit: David states his 'head hurts' and he has had a runny nose for 2 days, temperature is 100.3	
Current Medications: Amoxil 500mg three times daily for 10 days by mouth Also, see attached complete medication list.	
Staff Signature: Sam Dowd	**Date:** March 3, yr
Health Care Provider Findings: Sinus infection	
Medication/Treatment Orders: DC Amoxil ⟶ EES 666mg three times daily for 10 days by mouth	
Instructions: Call HCP if temperature remains elevated above 100.3 for more than 48 hours	
Follow-up visit:	**Lab work or Tests:** None today
Signature: Richard Black, MD	**Date:** March 3, yr

Posted by: Date: Time: Verified by: Date: Time:

Rx # 156	**Greenleaf Pharmacy** **20 Main Street** **Treetop, MA 09111**	**111-222-3434** **3/3/yr**
Generic ⟶ **David Cook** **Erythromycin 333mg** Brand ⟶ **IC EES** **Take 2 tablets by mouth three times daily for 10 days**		**Qty.60**
Dr. Black **Lot # 14239**	**ED: 3/3/yr**	**Refills: 0**

Massachusetts | Responsibilities in Action   97

2020 The Massachusetts Departments of Public Health, Developmental Services, Mental Health, Children and Families and the Rehabilitation Commission

When transcribing information onto the medication sheet it is important to understand that you must copy the dose from the HCP order and strength and amount must be copied from the pharmacy label.

The dose is copied from the HCP order and is copied next to the word dose on the medication sheet.

HEALTH CARE PROVIDER ORDER

Name: David Cook	**Date:** March 3, yr
Health Care Provider: Dr. Black	**Allergies:** No Known Allergies
Reason for Visit: David states his 'head hurts' and he has had a runny nose for 2 days, temperature is 100.3	
Current Medications: Amoxil 500mg three times daily for 10 days by mouth Also, see attached complete medication list.	
Staff Signature: Sam Dowd	**Date:** March 3, yr
Health Care Provider Findings: Sinus infection	
Medication/Treatment Orders: DC Amoxil Start EES 666mg three times daily for 10 days by mouth	
Instructions: Call HCP if temperature remains elevated above 100.3 for more than 48 hours	
Follow-up Visit:	**Lab work or Tests:** None today
Signature: Richard Black, MD	**Date:** March 3, yr

Posted by: Date: Time: Verified by: Date: Time

Start	Generic		Hour	1	2	3	4	5	6	7	8	9	10	11	12	13	14	15	16	17	18	19	20	21	22	23	24	25	26	27	28	29	30	31
	Brand																																
	Strength	Dose 666mg																															
Stop	Amount	Route																															
	Frequency																																

Special instructions: *Reason:*

Massachusetts | Responsibilities in Action   98

The strength and amount are copied from the pharmacy label.

The strength on a pharmacy label is usually next to or underneath the name of the medication, and is copied next to the word strength on the medication sheet.

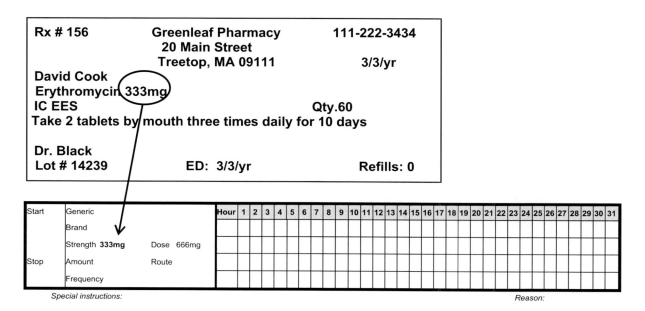

The amount on a pharmacy label is in the label directions and is copied next to the word amount on the medication sheet.

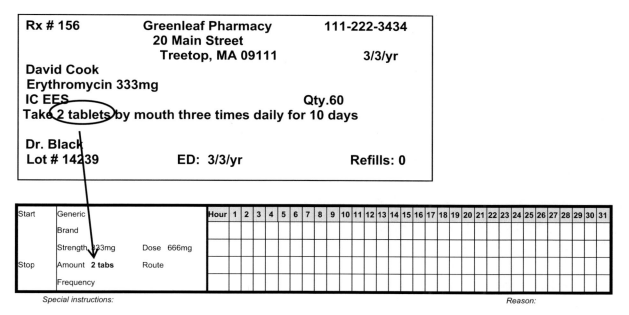

The medication name(s), frequency, route and any special instructions or parameters for use may be found on the HCP order and/or the pharmacy label and copied onto the left side of the medication sheet.

Start	Generic **Erythromycin**	Hour	1	2	3	4	5	6	7	8	9	10	11	12	13	14	15	16	17	18	19	20	21	22	23	24	25	26	27	28	29	30	31
	Brand **EES**																																	
	Strength **333mg** Dose **666mg**																																	
Stop	Amount **2 tabs** Route **Mouth**																																	
	Frequency **Three times daily**																																	

Special instructions: **for 10 days**   *Reason:* **Sinus infection**

If the medication name on the HCP order is written as a
- generic medication and the pharmacy supplies the generic medication then only the generic name of the medication is required to be transcribed onto the medication sheet
- brand name medication and the HCP includes 'brand only, no substitutions' on the prescription, the pharmacist will prepare the brand name medication and not the generic form. In this situation there will only be a brand name listed on the pharmacy label. Only the brand name (as listed on the HCP order and pharmacy label) will be transcribed onto the medication sheet.

The number of times per day the medication is ordered is copied next to the word 'frequency' on the medication sheet.

In addition to the number of times per day, if a specific number of days are also ordered, this information may also be written next to the word 'frequency' on the medication sheet if space allows and the information is legible.

If there is not enough space to print clearly, the specific number of days ordered may be copied in the special instructions area.

To complete the grid, follow these steps:

- Assign times in the hour column; times assigned should be at least 4 hours apart
  - For David, the HCP ordered the frequency as
    - Three times a day for 10 days.
  - Three 'times' are chosen and written in the hour column; 8am, 4pm and 8pm are examples of times often chosen.

- Think about the date and time to determine when the first dose can be administered
  - For David, based on the date and time, March 3, yr at 1pm:
    - The March 3rd 8am dose cannot be administered. The March 3rd 8am medication box is crossed (X) out; as are all boxes before it.
    - The medication can be administered March 3rd at 4pm, this medication box is left open and all boxes before it are crossed (X) out.
    - The medication can be administered March 3rd at 8pm, this medication box is left open and all boxes before it are crossed (X) out.

Start	Generic **Erythromycin**			Hour	1	2	3	4	5	6	7	8	9	10	11	12	13	14	15	16	17	18	19	20	21	22	23	24	25	26	27	28	29	30	31
	Brand **EES**			8am	X	X	X																												
	Strength **333mg**	Dose **666mg**																																
Stop	Amount **2 tabs**	Route **Mouth**		4pm	X	X																													
	Frequency **Three times daily**			8pm	X	X																													

Special instructions: **for 10 days**   *Reason:* **Sinus infection**

Next,

- If the medication is ordered to be administered for a certain number of days, the days must be counted
  - For David, the HCP ordered the medication to be administered for 10 days
    - For each scheduled time (8am, 4pm and 8pm), ten medication boxes are counted and left open; the remaining medication boxes are crossed (X) out.
- Write the 'start' and 'stop' dates:
  - A start date is the date the first dose is scheduled to be administered.
  - A stop date is the date the last dose is scheduled to be administered.

Start	Generic **Erythromycin**			Hour	1	2	3	4	5	6	7	8	9	10	11	12	13	14	15	16	17	18	19	20	21	22	23	24	25	26	27	28	29	30	31
3/3/yr	Brand **EES**			8am	X	X	X											X	X	X	X	X	X	X	X	X	X	X	X	X	X	X	X	X
	Strength **333mg**	Dose **666mg**																																
Stop	Amount **2 tabs**	Route **Mouth**		4pm	X	X													X	X	X	X	X	X	X	X	X	X	X	X	X	X	X	X	X
3/13/yr	Frequency **Three times daily**			8pm	X	X													X	X	X	X	X	X	X	X	X	X	X	X	X	X	X	X	X

Special instructions: **for 10 days**   *Reason:* **Sinus infection**

Massachusetts | Responsibilities in Action

This is the completed transcription of David Cook's HCP order and pharmacy label onto a medication sheet:

Month and Year: March, yr   MEDICATION ADMINISTRATION SHEET   Allergies: none

Start 2/28/yr	Generic **Amoxicillin** Brand **Amoxil** ~~DC 3/3/yr SD~~	Hour	1	2	3	4	5	6	7	8	9	10	11	12	13	14	15	16	17	18	19	20	21	22	23	24	25	26	27	28	29	30	31
	Strength **250mg** Dose **500mg**	8am	SW	AS	SW																													
Stop	Amount **2 tabs** Route **Mouth**	4pm	LW	JS																													
3/10/yr	Frequency **Three times daily**	8pm	LW	JS																													
	Special instructions: **for 10 days**																												Reason: **Sinus infection**				

(All subsequent cells marked with X indicating doses; DC 3/3/yr SD annotated across rows)

Start 3/3/yr	Generic **Erythromycin** Brand **EES**	Hour	1	2	3	4	5	6	7	8	9	10	11	12	13	14	15	16	17	18	19	20	21	22	23	24	25	26	27	28	29	30	31
	Strength **333mg** Dose **666mg**	8am	X	X	X							X	X	X	X	X	X	X	X	X	X	X	X	X	X	X	X	X	X	X	X		
Stop	Amount **2 tabs** Route **Mouth**	4pm	X	X									X	X	X	X	X	X	X	X	X	X	X	X	X	X	X	X	X	X	X		
3/13/yr	Frequency **Three times daily**	8pm	X	X									X	X	X	X	X	X	X	X	X	X	X	X	X	X	X	X	X	X	X		
	Special instructions: **for 10 days**																												Reason: **Sinus infection**				

(Third and fourth medication blocks are blank)

	CODES		Signature		Signature
Name: **David Cook**	DP-day program/day hab	SD	Sam Dowd		
	LOA-leave of absence	AS	*Amanda Smith*		
Site: **45 Shade Street**	P-packaged	LW	Linda White		
	W-work	SW	Serena Wilson		
	H-hospital, nursing home, rehab center	JS	Jenna Sherman		
	S-school				

Accuracy Check 1 *Linda White* Date 2/28/yr Time 8pm   Accuracy Check 2 Jenna Sherman Date 2/28/yr Time 8pm

Review the completed EES transcription and answer the following questions.

1. What is the date and time of the first scheduled dose of EES? _____

2. What is the 'start' date? _____

3. What is the date and time of the last scheduled dose of EES? _____

4. What is the 'stop' date? _____

5. What is the frequency? _____

6. What are the times the medication is scheduled to be administered? _____

7. What is the dose of the new medication? _____

8. What is the amount to administer? _____

9. What is the strength of the tablet supplied? _____

10. What is the name of the staff that transcribed the order? _____

Electronic health records are another method of recording medication administration. If this is the method used in your work location, ask your Supervisor when you will receive training.

If anything about an existing HCP order changes (frequency, dose, parameters for use etc.), it is considered to be a new HCP order. The old HCP order must be discontinued on the medication sheet and the new HCP order transcribed.

Posting and Verifying

After a HCP order is transcribed onto a medication sheet, the HCP order is Posted and Verified. Posting and Verifying is completed by two Certified and/or licensed staff. Posting is documentation of the staff that completed the transcription.

After all orders are transcribed, the first staff documents:

- 'Posted'
    - on the HCP order form
    - under the HCP's signature
- Date
- Time
- Staff signature

To verify an order, the second staff must review the transcription completed by the first staff, ensuring the HCP order and pharmacy label information was accurately transcribed onto the medication sheet.

Massachusetts | Responsibilities in Action 103

The second staff documents:

- 'Verified'
  - on the HCP order form
  - under the HCP's signature
- Date
- Time
- Staff signature

Posting and verifying helps to ensure all medication orders are transcribed accurately onto medication sheets so that medication is administered as ordered.

All HCP orders must be posted and verified including when the HCP notes, 'no new orders' or 'no medication changes'.

If two Certified and/or licensed staff are not available when the medication is due to be administered, the first staff completes the transcription and posts the HCP order. After posting, the medication may be administered by the Certified and/or licensed staff that posted the order. The next staff on duty must verify the order before administering any further doses

Staff must document that there was a new HCP order in the person's health record.

Note the HCP order has been posted and verified under the HCP signature.

HEALTH CARE PROVIDER ORDER

Name: David Cook	**Date:** March 3, yr
Health Care Provider: Dr. Black	**Allergies:** No Known Allergies
Reason for Visit: David states his 'head hurts' and he has had a runny nose for 2 days, temperature is 100.3	
Current Medications: Amoxil 500mg three times daily for 10 days by mouth Also, see attached complete medication list.	
Staff Signature: Sam Dowd	**Date:** March 3, yr
Health Care Provider Findings: Sinus infection	
Medication/Treatment Orders: Amoxil EES 666mg three times daily for 10 days by mouth	
Instructions: Call HCP if temperature remains elevated above 100.3 for more than 48 hours	
Follow-up visit:	**Lab work or Tests:** None today
Signature: Richard Black, MD	**Date:** March 3, yr

Posted by: **Sam Dowd** Date: 3/3/yr Time: 1:15pm Verified by: Linda White Date: 3/3/yr Time: 2pm

Telephone orders are different in that once the medication is received from the pharmacy, after transcribing, the orders are posted and verified twice:

- First when the order is initially obtained
- Again after the HCP has signed the order, ensuring there were no changes

Tanisha has returned from a HCP appointment and medication has been obtained from the pharmacy. The date is February 5th, yr. The time is 1pm. Use the HCP order, pharmacy label and medication sheet to transcribe the new orders. Remember to post the HCP order after completing the transcription.

HEALTH CARE PROVIDER ORDER

Name: Tanisha Johnson	Date: Feb. 5, yr
Health Care Provider: Dr. Chen Lee	Allergies: No known medication allergies
Reason for Visit: Continues to complain of soreness in back of mouth	
Current Medications: Phenobarbital 64.8mg once daily in the evening by mouth Clonazepam 1mg twice daily at 8am and 4pm by mouth Amoxil Suspension 500mg every 12 hours for seven days by mouth	
Staff Signature: Sam Dowd	Date: Feb. 5, yr
Health Care Provider Findings: Increased inflammation of gum-line on left side of mouth	
Medication/Treatment Orders: DC Amoxil Suspension Cleocin HCL 300mg three times a day for 10 days by mouth	
Instructions: Notify HCP if Tanisha continues to complain of mouth soreness after 72 hours.	
Follow-up visit: February 16, yr	Lab work or Tests: None
Signature: Dr. Chen Lee	Date: Feb. 5, yr

Posted by: Date: Time: Verified by: Date: Time:

Rx #178 — Greenleaf Pharmacy

Rx #178

Greenleaf Pharmacy
20 Main Street
Treetop, MA 00000

111-222-3434

2/5/yr

Tanisha Johnson

Clindamycin 100mg
IC Cleocin HCL

Qty. 90

Take 3 tablets by mouth 3 times a day for 10 days
Take with 8 ounces of water

Lot# 352   **ED: 2/5/yr**

Dr. Lee
Refills: 0

Month and Year: February, yr   **MEDICATION ADMINISTRATION SHEET**   **Allergies: none**

		Hour	1	2	3	4	5	6	7	8	9	10	11	12	13	14	15	16	17	18	19	20	21	22	23	24	25	26	27	28	29	30	31
Start 8/31/yr	Generic Phenobarbital Brand Luminal Strength 32.4mg Dose 64.8mg																																
Stop Cont.	Amount 2 tabs Route Mouth Frequency Once daily in evening	8pm TM TM TM JS																															

Special instructions: — Reason: seizures

		Hour	1	2	3	4	5	6	7	8	9	10	11	12	13	14	15	16	17	18	19	20	21	22	23	24	25	26	27	28	29	30	31
Start 8/31/yr	Generic Clonazepam Brand Klonopin Strength 1mg Dose 1mg	8am KM AS KM KM AS																															
Stop Cont.	Amount 1 tab Route Mouth Frequency Twice daily 8am and 4pm	4pm TM TM TM JS																															

Special instructions: — Reason: seizures

		Hour	1	2	3	4	5	6	7	8	9	10	11	12	13	14	15	16	17	18	19	20	21	22	23	24	25	26	27	28	29	30	31
Start 2/2/yr	Generic Amoxicillin suspension Brand Amoxil suspension Strength 250mg/5mL Dose 500mg	8am X X KM KM AS	X	X	X	X	X	X	X	X	X	X	X	X	X	X	X	X	X	X	X	X	X	X	X	X	X	X
Stop 2/9/yr	Amount 10mL Route Mouth Frequency every 12 hours for 7 days	8pm X TM TM JS	X	X	X	X	X	X	X	X	X	X	X	X	X	X	X	X	X	X	X	X	X	X	X	X	X	X	X

Special instructions: — Reason: gum inflammation

		Hour	1	2	3	4	5	6	7	8	9	10	11	12	13	14	15	16	17	18	19	20	21	22	23	24	25	26	27	28	29	30	31
Start	Generic Brand Strength Dose																																
Stop	Amount Route Frequency																																

Special instructions: — Reason:

CODES			Signature			Signature
DP-day program/day hab	KM	Kay Mathers		JC	John Craig	
LOA-leave of absence	AS	Amanda Smith				
P-packaged	TM	Timothy Miller				
W-work	SW	Serena Wilson				
H-hospital, nursing home, rehab center	JS	Jenna Sherman				
S-school	SD	Sam Dowd				

Name: Tanisha Johnson

Site: 45 Shade Street
Treetop MA 00000

Accuracy Check 1 Sam Dowd   Date 1/31/yr   Time 9pm   Accuracy Check 2 John Craig   Date 1/31/yr   Time 9pm

2020 The Massachusetts Departments of Public Health, Developmental Services, Mental Health, Children and Families and the Rehabilitation Commission

Answer the following questions by choosing the best response.

1. Sam Dowd has written his initials and signed his full name on the signature list of a person's medication sheet. This is done

    A. __ every time he administers a medication
    B. __ once each month to identify his initials with his full name
    C. __ at the beginning of each shift
    D. __ only when he administers a PRN medication

2. Sam Dowd documented 'DP', in a medication box on the medication sheet. This indicates that the person

    A. __ received their daily pills
    B. __ refused all afternoon medications
    C. __ was at the day program when the medication was due
    D. __ is at a doctor's appointment and is unable to take medication

3. When transcribing the dose onto the medication sheet

    A. __ copy it from the pharmacy label
    B. __ multiply the amount sent by the pharmacy
    C. __ locate it on the HCP order
    D. __ divide the strength of the tablet by the amount to give

4. The start date for a medication

    A. __ will always be the date the medication was ordered
    B. __ is located on the HCP order
    C. __ is the date a person receives the first scheduled dose
    D. __ is listed on the pharmacy label

5. The allergy information on a medication sheet

    A. __ only needs to be filled in if a person has an allergy
    B. __ must be completed; if the person has no allergies list "none"
    C. __ must be written in red, highlighted and initialed by the supervisor
    D. __ can be written under special instructions

Medication Information Sheets

The last section of the medication record typically contains the medication information sheets. Medication information sheets can be obtained from the pharmacy printed from a reputable online resource or can be found packaged with the medication as an insert.

Remember you must learn about a medication before administering it.

Let's Review

- A medication sheet is a document used to track the administration of a person's medication
- The HCP order and pharmacy label are needed to complete a transcription
    - The dose is copied from the HCP order
    - The strength and amount are copied from the pharmacy label
- A specific time must be transcribed in the hour column on the medication sheet
- The start date is the date a person is scheduled to receive the first dose of a medication
- The stop date is the date a person is scheduled to receive the last dose of a medication
- Transcriptions must be completed accurately to ensure safe medication administration
- All HCP orders must be posted and verified to ensure HCP orders are accurately transcribed onto the medication sheet
    - All HCP orders must be posted and verified even if no new orders or medication changes have been written. This is documentation that staff are aware that no changes have been made.
- Accuracy checks must be completed, by two staff, prior to the start of the new month's medication sheets
- Medication information sheets are a valuable medication information resource

Unit 7

Administering Medications

Responsibilities you will learn

- The difference between regularly scheduled and as needed (PRN) medications
- The medication administration process
- How to use liquid medication measuring devices
- How to manage various scenarios if a medication is not administered

It is important to know the difference between which medications you will administer regularly and which medications you will administer only if needed. Regularly scheduled medications are ordered and administered due to various health conditions such as high blood pressure or high cholesterol. They are typically taken every day at routine time(s) in order to work as intended.

However, other medications are ordered and are only administered as needed for specific health issues if they occur such as chest pain, seasonal allergies, cold symptoms or constipation. These medications are only administered on an 'as needed' or 'PRN' basis.

Regularly Scheduled Medications

Regularly scheduled medications are administered routinely, on a continuing basis.

For example: Colace 100mg twice daily by mouth

In the example, the medication will be administered twice daily at two specific times, as listed under the hour column on the medication sheet.

Start	Generic **Docusate Sodium**	Hour	1	2	3	4	5	6	7	8	9	10	11	12	13	14	15	16	17	18	19	20	21	22	23	24	25	26	27	28	29	30	31
8/31/yr	Brand **Colace**	8am	WS	AM	JC	WS																												
	Strength **100mg** Dose **100mg**																																	
Stop	Amount **1 tab** Route **Mouth**																																	
Cont.	Frequency **Twice daily**	8pm	SD	SD	KM	KM																												

Special instructions: *Reason:* **constipation**

When data collection is required for medication administration, such as vital signs or bowel tracking, the data must be recorded on the medication sheet, above or below the medication to be administered.

Review the medication sheet. What is the data being recorded? _____

Start 8/31/yr Stop Cont.	Generic Brand **Check blood pressure (BP)** Strength Dose Amount Route Frequency **Daily in the morning**	Hour 1 2 3 4 5 6 7 8 9 10 11 12 13 14 15 16 17 18 19 20 21 22 23 24 25 26 27 28 29 30 31 8am WS AS JC WS BP 120/64 134/66 130/62 132/60

Special instructions: **Hold Zestril if systolic (top) blood pressure (BP) reading is below 100 and notify HCP**   Reason:

Start 8/31/yr Stop Cont.	Generic **Lisinopril** Brand **Zestril** Strength **20mg** Dose **40mg** Amount **2 tabs** Route **Mouth** Frequency **Daily in the morning**	Hour 1 2 3 4 5 6 7 8 9 10 11 12 13 14 15 16 17 18 19 20 21 22 23 24 25 26 27 28 29 30 31 8am WS AS JC WS

Special instructions: **Hold Zestril if systolic (top) blood pressure (BP) reading is below 100 and notify HCP**   Reason: **high BP**

Certified staff must be trained in vital sign (VS) monitoring as it relates to medication administration. A HCP, RN, LPN, pharmacist, paramedic or EMT must conduct Vital Signs training.

Ask your Supervisor if there are people who have HCP orders requiring vital sign monitoring at your work location and if so, when you will be trained.

PRN Medications

Medications that are administered only 'as needed' are known and abbreviated as 'PRN'. In addition to including the 5 rights of medication administration, PRN medication orders must also include the following details:

- The specific target signs and symptoms for use such as
    - complaint of 'headache'
    - no bowel movement in 3 days
    - complaint of right knee discomfort

Massachusetts | Responsibilities in Action

- Measurable objective criteria, if needed, such as
  - head slapping for more than 5 minutes
  - seizure lasting more than 1 minute
  - temperature of 101 or more
- A PRN frequency
  - How many hours apart the doses may be administered such as
    - 'every 8 hours PRN' or
    - three times daily PRN, must separate doses by at least 6 hours or
    - how many hours apart are required between a PRN dose and a regularly scheduled dose of the same medication, such as
      - 'Do not give within 4 hours of a regularly scheduled dose'
- Parameters for use
  - How many doses of medication may be administered before the HCP must be notified such as
    - 'If 4 doses are administered within 24 hours, notify the HCP'
  - What to do if the medication is administered and is not effective such as
    - 'If complaints of right knee pain continues longer than 2 hours after PRN medication is administered, notify the HCP'

A PRN medication may only be administered for the target signs and symptoms ordered by the HCP. Remember, target signs and symptoms ordered by the HCP indicate 'when' you should administer a PRN medication. A reason is 'why' a medication is ordered by the HCP. For example, Tylenol is ordered for fever (reason); it is administered if temperature is over 101 (target sign/symptom).

PRN medication orders must include specific target signs and symptoms and instructions for use including what to do if the medication is given and is not effective.

For example, Tanisha has an order for:

Milk of Magnesia 1200mg by mouth PRN every 3rd evening if no bowel movement (BM). Contact HCP if no BM by the next morning.

On the medication sheet under the hour column you will see the abbreviation 'PRN'. Specific to this example, to follow the order as written, BM data must be cross-referenced; this includes during day program or work hours. You will look for the BM

Massachusetts | Responsibilities in Action 113

data documented on the medication sheet to determine whether or not the medication must be administered.

Based on the bowel data tracking entered (which includes day program data), does the Milk of Magnesia require administration on the evening of the 5th? _____

Start	Generic **Monitor and record number**	Hour	1	2	3	4	5	6	7	8	9	10	11	12	13	14	15	16	17	18	19	20	21	22	23	24	25	26	27	28	29	30	31
6/1/yr	Brand **of bowel movements (BM)**	7-3	0	1	0	0	0																											
	Strength — Dose	3-11	1	1	0	0	0																											
Stop	Amount — Route	11-7	0	0	0	0	0																											
Cont.	Frequency **Every shift**																																	

Special instructions: **Check daily Monday-Friday with day program and record**　　　*Reason:*

Start	Generic **Magnesium hydroxide**	Hour	1	2	3	4	5	6	7	8	9	10	11	12	13	14	15	16	17	18	19	20	21	22	23	24	25	26	27	28	29	30	31
6/1/yr	Brand **Milk of Magnesia**	P																																
	Strength **400mg/5mL** Dose **1200mg**	R																																
Stop	Amount **15mL** Route **Mouth**	N																																
Cont.	Frequency **PRN every 3rd evening if no BM**																																	

Special instructions: **Contact HCP if no bowel movement by the next morning.**　　　*Reason:* **Constipation**

A PRN medication is documented on a medication sheet by

- writing your initials and the time administered, in the same medication box
  - across from the medication administered,
    - under the correct date.
  - if the medication is administered in the morning, use one of the top two medication grid boxes on the medication sheet.
  - if administered in the afternoon or evening (as ordered in the example above); document using one of the two bottom medication grid boxes.
- You will also write a corresponding medication progress note including
  - the date and time
  - medication and dose administered
  - the reason administered
  - your signature
    - After enough time has passed, typically no sooner than 1 hour after administration, document the results and/or response to the medication
      - Use a new line in the progress notes, if needed

Massachusetts | Responsibilities in Action　114

Example of PRN medication documentation:

Start 8/31/yr	Generic **Ibuprofen**																																		
	Brand **Motrin**	Hour	1	2	3	4	5	6	7	8	9	10	11	12	13	14	15	16	17	18	19	20	21	22	23	24	25	26	27	28	29	30	31
	Strength **400mg** Dose **400mg**	P																																
Stop	Amount **1 tab** Route **Mouth**	R																																
Cont.	Frequency **Every 8 hours as needed**	N	3pm AS																														

Special instructions: **for complaint of right knee pain. Notify HCP if pain continues after 48 hours**   Reason: **right knee pain**

Name   **David Cook**   **MEDICATION PROGRESS NOTE**   **March, yr**

Date	Time	Medication	Dose	Given	Not Given	Refused	Other	Reason (for giving/not giving)	Results and/or Response	Staff Signature
3/1/yr	3pm	Ibuprofen	400mg	X				David states, 'my right knee hurts'.		*Amanda Smith*
3/1/yr	4pm	At 4pm David says, 'It still hurts to bend my knee.'								*Amanda Smith*

Review the HCP order for David Cook and answer the questions.

Health Care Provider Order

Motrin 400mg every 8 hours as needed by mouth for complaints of right knee pain Notify HCP if symptoms continue for more than 48 hours.

1. Is the Motrin ordered as a regularly scheduled or PRN medication? _____

2. What is the reason the medication is ordered? _____

3. Are you allowed to administer the Motrin if he complains of a headache? _____

4. If administered at 9am, what is the earliest time it may be administered again? __

5. If the medication has been administered as ordered for 48 hours and David still complains of right knee pain, what should you do? _____

The 5 Rights of Medication Administration

To ensure medications are administered safely, each time you administer medication you will compare the 5 rights of medication administration between the HCP order, the pharmacy label and the medication sheet. The 5 rights of medication administration are the:

- Right Person
- Right Medication
- Right Dose
- Right Time
- Right Route

Right Person

To be sure you have the right person the person's name on the HCP order, the pharmacy label and the medication sheet must agree. If you are not sure who the person is never ask their name as a way of identification, such as 'Are you David Cook?' The reason is because, someone other than David may respond.

- Know that you can identify the right person by
  - o Asking a staff who is familiar with the person or
  - o Looking at a current picture of the person

Once you identify the right person, locate the person's name written on the HCP order, the person's name printed on the pharmacy label and the person's name transcribed on the medication sheet. If the names are different, you will contact a MAP Consultant.

Many times medication records are organized to include a person's Emergency Fact Sheet, which includes a picture of the person that can be used to identify the right person; followed by the HCP order, medication sheet and medication information sheet.

Name						Nickname		
David Cook						Dave		

Current Address
45 Shade Street, Treetop MA 00000

Former Address
25 Smith Street, Oldtown MA 00000

Sex	Race	D.O.B.	Age*	Height*	Weight*	Build	Hair	Eyes
M	Cauc	3-15-64	52	6'1"	196		Br	Bl

Distinguishing Marks
Mole on right shoulder

Legal Competency Status
Presumed Competent

If Legal Guardian, Name / **Phone**
NA

Address / **Work**

Family Address (if different) / **Phone**
25 Smith Street — 617-000-0000

Oldtown MA 00000

Training / Work Program	Address	Phone
Amercare Services	13 Main Street Treetop MA 00000	617-000-0000

Relevant Emergency Medical Information: (Allergies, Medications, etc.)

Allergies-none
Diagnoses-High blood pressure, osteoarthritis right knee, GERD, Down Syndrome, Sleep Apnea and Constipation

Physician's Name	Address	Phone
Dr. Richard Black	504 Lyman Street, Treetop MA 00000	617-000-0000

Language / Communication / **Ability to protect self w/o assistance**
Speaks and understands English
Minimal ability to read and write — yes

Significant Behavior Characteristics / **Likely Response To Search Efforts**
none — good

Pattern of Movement (if lost previously) / **Places Frequented**

Relevant Capabilities: / **Limitations:** / **Preferences:**
Independent with ADLs — Enjoys riding on buses

Probable Dress*

Where and When the person was last seen / **Date*** / **Time***

Emergency Contacts

FAMILY / GUARDIAN	David Cook, Sr. (father)	DDS	Sky Johnson, Service Coordinator
RESIDENCE	Linda White, Program Manager		

Note: Asterisked (*) items are left blank on the original and filled in on copy if and when the individual is lost. Except age, height, and weight which must be reported at all times on the form.

NAME	COMMONWEALTH OF MASSACHUSETTS	AREA
David Cook		Anywhere Area Office
RECORD LOCATION		
45 Shade Street	**EMERGENCY**	
Treetop MA 00000	**FACT SHEET**	

2020 The Massachusetts Departments of Public Health, Developmental Services, Mental Health, Children and Families and the Rehabilitation Commission

Massachusetts | Responsibilities in Action

Right Medication

To be sure you have the right medication, the medication name on the HCP order, the pharmacy label and the medication sheet must agree. Read each medication name to ensure it matches letter for letter. Each medication usually has a brand and a generic name.

- Know that when identifying the right medication
  - o if a brand name medication is written on the HCP order, it will typically be substituted by the pharmacy with the generic medication.
- You will see
  - o the brand name on the HCP order
  - o both the brand and generic names on the pharmacy label
  - o both the brand and generic names on the medication sheet

Once you identify the right medication, locate the medication name(s) written on the HCP order, the medication name(s) printed on the pharmacy label and the medication name(s) transcribed on the medication sheet. If the medication names are different, you will contact a MAP Consultant.

Many medications come in different formulations that have similar names. For example Depakote DR (Delayed Release), Depakote EC (Enteric Coated) and Depakote ER (Extended Release) are different forms of Depakote that can be easily confused. Make sure that the HCP order, pharmacy label and medication sheet match for the specific medication formulation.

Massachusetts | Responsibilities in Action

Compare the 5 rights between the HCP order and the pharmacy label. Do the 5 rights agree? ___ If no, why _____

HEALTH CARE PROVIDER ORDER

Name: Scott Green	**Date:** March 3, yr
Health Care Provider: Dr. Glass	**Allergies:** No Known Allergies
Reason for Visit: Annual physical exam	
Current Medications: See attached medication list.	
Staff Signature: Tom *Salowsky*	**Date:** March 3, yr
Health Care Provider Findings: Start Aspirin EC as preventive measure secondary to diabetes	
Medication/Treatment Orders: Aspirin EC 81mg by mouth once daily in the morning	
Instructions:	
Follow-up visit:	**Lab work or Tests:** CMP and CBC
Signature: *Shirley Glass MD*	**Date:** March 3, yr

Rx #555	**Greenleaf Pharmacy** 20 Main Street Treetop, MA 00000	**111-222-3434** 3/3/yr
Scott Green		
Aspirin 81mg		**Qty. 30**
Take 1 tablet by mouth once daily in the morning		
Lot# 777	**ED: 3/3/yr**	**Dr. Glass** **Refills: 5**

Massachusetts | Responsibilities in Action   119

Right Dose

To be sure you have the right dose, the dose written on the HCP order, the pharmacy label and the medication sheet must agree. The dose is how much medication the HCP orders the person to receive each time it is scheduled to be administered.

- Know that when identifying the right dose you will see the
  - dose on the HCP order
    - The number is most often written in milligrams, 'mg'
  - strength of the tablet and the amount of tablets to administer on the pharmacy label
  - dose, strength and amount on the medication sheet

The dose ordered by the HCP will equal the strength of a tablet, multiplied by the amount to administer, as printed in the pharmacy label directions.

As you begin to administer medication you will notice the strength of the tablet supplied by the pharmacy can be

- the same as the dose ordered or
- a different number and when multiplied by the amount to administer will equal the dose ordered.

Dose = Strength X Amount

The HCP orders the dose of a medication.

Health Care Provider Order

Name:	Date:
Health Care Provider:	Allergies:
Reason for Visit:	
Current Medications:	
Staff Signature:	Date:
Health Care Provider Findings:	
Medication/Treatment Orders:	
Instructions:	
Follow-up visit:	Lab work or Tests:
Signature:	Date:

Dose ordered is 100mg

The pharmacy supplies the strength of the tablet and label directions for the amount to give to equal the dose ordered. The strength supplied and the amount to give can change; the dose ordered remains the same.

Dose		Strength	Amount
100mg	=	25mg 25mg 25mg 25mg	4 tablets
100mg	=	50mg 50mg	2 tablets
100mg	=	100mg	1 tablet
100mg	=	200mg, ½ tablet	½ tablet

Massachusetts | Responsibilities in Action

Review the dose of medication ordered by the HCP, the strength of the tablet supplied by the pharmacy and fill in the amount of tablet(s) or capsule(s) to administer you would expect to see printed in the pharmacy label directions.

	Dose	Strength	Amount
1.	100mg	50mg tablet	
2.	150mg	75mg tablet	
3.	500mg	250mg capsule	
4.	375mg	125mg tablet	
5.	500mg	500mg capsule	
6.	4mg	1mg tablet	
7.	10mg	2mg tablet	
8.	60mg	30mg capsule	
9.	600/200mg	300/100mg tablet	
10.	25mg	12.5mg tablet	
11.	12.5mg	25mg tablet	

Once you identify the right dose, locate the dose written on the HCP order, the strength of the tablet and the amount to administer printed on the pharmacy label and the dose, strength and amount transcribed on the medication sheet. If the dose does not agree, you will contact a MAP Consultant.

Right Time

To be sure you have the right time, the time written on the HCP order, the pharmacy label and medication sheet must agree. The words frequency and time are used interchangeably.

- Know that when identifying the right time the
  - HCP will order how many times throughout a day a medication is to be administered
  - pharmacy label directions will include the frequency
  - medication sheet includes the frequency as ordered by the HCP and
    - The specific times chosen are written under the hour column on the medication sheet

Once you identify the right time, locate the frequency written in the HCP order, the frequency printed on the pharmacy label and the frequency transcribed on the medication sheet. If the frequencies are different, you will contact a MAP Consultant.

All medications must be administered 'on time'. On time is defined as one hour before the time chosen in the hour column on the medication sheet up to one hour after the time chosen in the hour column on the medication sheet.

The one-hour window does not apply to PRN medication. PRN medication is administered when the target signs and symptoms are met, based on the frequency ordered. If you are unsure, contact a MAP Consultant.

Right Route

To be sure you have the right route, the route written on the HCP order, the pharmacy label and the medication sheet must agree. The route is the way medication enters the body.

- Know that the
    - HCP order will include the route
    - pharmacy label directions will include the route
    - medication sheet will include the route

Once you identify the right route, locate the route written in the HCP order, the route printed on the pharmacy label and the route transcribed on the medication sheet. If the routes are different, you will contact a MAP Consultant.

Medication administered orally (by mouth) is the focus of this training. If a person is unable to take medications by mouth or if the medication is not available in oral form (tablets, capsules, liquids), medications can enter the body by other routes. Other routes include, but are not limited to:

Route	Definition
Buccal	Placed in the cheek
Enteral	Administration into the stomach or intestines by gtube or jtube
Inhalable	Inhaled orally or nasally
Intramuscular	Administration in a muscle
Nasal	Administration in the nose by spray or pump
Ophthalmic	Administration in the eye
Otic	Administration in the ear
Rectal	Administration to or in the rectum
Subcutaneous	Administration between the skin and the muscle
Sublingual	Placed under the tongue
Topical	Applied directly to the skin
Transdermal	Administration through the skin
Vaginal	Administration to or in the vagina

Massachusetts | Responsibilities in Action

Never administer a medication by a route for which you have not received training. Your supervisor will arrange for an RN, an LPN or a MAP Trainer who has the necessary knowledge, skills and abilities to conduct additional route training, when needed.

Specialized training is required if a person receives:

- Medication through enteral routes, i.e., a gastrostomy or jejunostomy (g/j) tube.
- Auto injectable epinephrine, such as an EpiPen or an Auvi-Q through the intramuscular route.

You are newly Certified. You know a person in your work location has an order for an EpiPen. Before you are assigned medication administration duties you should

1. ___ Ask a coworker to show you how it is administered
2. ___ Call the pharmacy and ask for instructions
3. ___ Read the medication information sheet so you will know how to use it
4. ___ Ask your Supervisor to arrange a specialized training for EpiPen use

Ask your Supervisor when you will receive training on all other routes medications are administered in your work location.

You will be comparing the 5 rights between the HCP order, the pharmacy label and the medication sheet as you complete 3 checks to ensure safe medication administration.

Massachusetts | Responsibilities in Action 125

2020 The Massachusetts Departments of Public Health, Developmental Services, Mental Health, Children and Families and the Rehabilitation Commission

The 3 Checks of Medication Administration

The 3 checks of medication administration are a comparison of the 5 rights. Compare the

1. HCP order and the pharmacy label (Check 1)
2. Pharmacy label and the medication sheet (Check 2)
3. Pharmacy label and the medication sheet (Check 3)

Check 1 is a comparison of the 5 rights between the HCP order and the pharmacy label:

Health Care Provider Order

Name:	Date:
Health Care Provider:	Allergies:
Reason for Visit:	
Current Medications:	
Staff Signature:	Date:
Health Care Provider Findings:	
Medication/Treatment Orders:	
Instructions:	
Follow-up visit:	Lab work or Tests:
Signature:	Date:

- The reason(s) for check 1 is to make sure
    - there is a HCP order for the medication you are going to administer
    - what the HCP ordered is what the pharmacy supplied and
    - the order has not changed since the last time you administered medication

Check 2 is a comparison of the 5 rights between the pharmacy label and the medication sheet:

Medication Sheet

- The reason(s) for check 2 is to make sure
  - the strength of each tablet supplied and the amount of tablets to administer printed on the pharmacy label agree with what is transcribed on the medication sheet and
  - that you focus on the number of tablets needed
- After check 2 you place the correct number of tablets in the medication cup

Check 3 is a comparison of the 5 rights between the pharmacy label and the medication sheet:

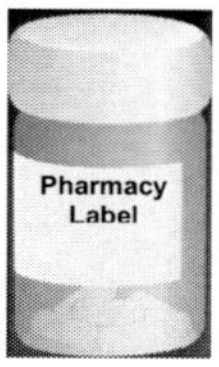

Medication Sheet

Start	Generic		Hour	1	2	3	4	5	6	7	8	9	10	11	12	13	14	15	16	17	18	19	20	21	22	23	24	25	26	27	28	29	30	31
	Brand																																	
	Strength	Dose																																
Stop	Amount	Route																																
	Frequency																																	

Special instructions: *Reason:*

Start	Generic		Hour	1	2	3	4	5	6	7	8	9	10	11	12	13	14	15	16	17	18	19	20	21	22	23	24	25	26	27	28	29	30	31
	Brand																																	
	Strength	Dose																																
Stop	Amount	Route																																
	Frequency																																	

Special instructions: *Reason:*

Start	Generic		Hour	1	2	3	4	5	6	7	8	9	10	11	12	13	14	15	16	17	18	19	20	21	22	23	24	25	26	27	28	29	30	31
	Brand																																	
	Strength	Dose																																
Stop	Amount	Route																																
	Frequency																																	

Special instructions: *Reason:*

Start	Generic		Hour	1	2	3	4	5	6	7	8	9	10	11	12	13	14	15	16	17	18	19	20	21	22	23	24	25	26	27	28	29	30	31
	Brand																																	
	Strength	Dose																																
Stop	Amount	Route																																
	Frequency																																	

Special instructions: *Reason:*

	CODES		Signature		Signature
Name:	DP-day program/day hab				
	LOA-leave of absence				
Site:	P-packaged				
	W-work				
	H-hospital, nursing home, rehab center				
	S-school				

- The reason for check 3 is to make sure you placed the correct number of tablets in the medication cup according to the pharmacy label directions and the amount transcribed on the medication sheet

- After check 3 you administer the medication

The standard when administering medication is to administer whole tablets or capsules with water.

Fill in the blanks using the terms 'HCP order', 'pharmacy label' and/or 'medication sheet'.

1. Check 1 is comparing the 5 rights between the _____ and the_____.

2. Check 2 is comparing the 5 rights between the _____ and the_____.

3. Check 3 is comparing the 5 rights between the _____ and the_____.

Match each check in the medication administration process to its corresponding reason.

Check 1_____   A. To ensure the instructions and amount to administer on the label agree with what is transcribed onto the medication sheet

Check 2_____   B. To verify that the amount of medication that you prepared is what the pharmacy label and medication sheet instruct

Check 3_____   C. To ensure the pharmacy supplied the medication as ordered by the HCP

Compare the 5 rights between the HCP order and the pharmacy label.   Do the 5 rights agree? ___ If no, why not?_____

HEALTH CARE PROVIDER ORDER

Name: David Cook	**Date:** March 3, yr
Health Care Provider: Dr. Black	**Allergies:** No Known Allergies
Reason for Visit: David states he has 'trouble going' when having a bowel movement.	
Current Medications: See attached medication list.	
Staff Signature: Sam Dowd	**Date:** March 3, yr
Health Care Provider Findings: constipation	
Medication/Treatment Orders: Colace 200mg by mouth once daily in evening	
Instructions:	
Follow-up visit:	**Lab work or Tests:** None
Signature: *Richard Black, MD*	**Date:** March 3, yr

Rx #201	**Greenleaf Pharmacy** **20 Main Street** **Treetop, MA 00000**	**111-222-3434** **3/3/yr**
David Cook		
Docusate sodium 100mg **IC Colace**		**Qty. 60**
Take 2 tablets by mouth every evening at 8pm		
Lot# 463	**ED: 3/3/yr**	**Dr. Black** **Refills: 5**

Massachusetts | Responsibilities in Action   131

Special Instructions

Look at the entire pharmacy labeled container to see if there are special instructions you must follow when preparing, administering or storing the medication, such as, 'do not crush', 'shake well' or 'refrigerate'.

There are people who have difficulty swallowing a whole tablet with water. In these cases, you must report this to the HCP. The HCP will determine if it is acceptable for you to change the form of a medication.

A HCP order is required to

- place the whole tablet or capsule in applesauce, yogurt or pudding, etc.
- crush the tablet and mix with applesauce, yogurt or pudding, etc.
- open the contents of a capsule and mix with applesauce, yogurt or pudding, etc.
- mix two liquid medications together
- mix crushed medication and liquid medication together
- dissolve the medication in water
- give the medication with a liquid other than water

If a tablet must be halved or quartered in order to administer the correct dose, it must be done by the pharmacy. You are not allowed to break, split or cut a tablet.

True (T) or False (F)

1. ____ You must contact the HCP to obtain an order if a person requests apple juice with their medication if no order exists.

2. ____ A tablet may only be halved or quartered by the pharmacy.

3. ____ You may place whole pills in applesauce, yogurt or pudding without an HCP order.

4. ____ Liquid medications may be mixed together if ordered by the HCP.

5. ____ A HCP order is not required to open a capsule and mix the contents with applesauce.

Medication Administration Process

Administering medication is part of a larger process called the Medication Administration Process. Medication is prepared and administered to one person at a time. The medication administration process includes what happens before, during and after you complete the 3 checks of the 5 rights. The process includes what you will do to:

- **Prepare**
- **Administer**
- **Complete**

Prepare

- Wash
    - the area
        - If a tabletop surface is used as you prepare medication make sure you wipe it clean before starting.
    - your hands
        - Proper hand washing includes wetting your hands with clean, running water and applying soap. Lather your hands by rubbing them together with the soap. Be sure to lather the backs of your hands, between your fingers, and under your nails. Rub your hands for at least 20 seconds. Rinse thoroughly and dry.
        -

- Unlock the storage area

- Review the medication administration sheet specific to any medication due to be administered

    - Take out the medication(s) to be administered

    - Locate the corresponding HCP order(s)

Be mindful, before you prepare, gather all necessary supplies and equipment; for example, a glass of water, spoons, medication cups and proper liquid measuring devices, etc.

Massachusetts | Responsibilities in Action 134

Administer

- Check 1
  - Compare the 5 rights on the HCP order to the 5 rights on the pharmacy label
- Check 2
  - Compare the 5 rights on the pharmacy label to the 5 rights on the medication sheet
- Place the correct number of tablets in the medication cup
  - When removing a tablet from a
    - blister pack
      - always start with the highest numbered 'bubble'; place the medication cup underneath firmly and push the tablet through the backing directly into the medication cup
    - bottle
      - the cap may have instructions to push down then turn or there may be arrows you must line up to remove the cap. Tap the number of tablets needed into the bottle cap then place directly into the medication cup
- Check 3
  - Compare the 5 rights on the pharmacy label to the 5 rights on the medication sheet
- Administer the medication
  - The medication is given directly from you to the person
  - Stay with the person until the medication is swallowed
- Look Back
  - Review the pharmacy label and medication sheet to make sure that what the person just swallowed is what you intended to administer
    - If you realize you made a mistake notify a MAP Consultant immediately

Complete

- Document
  - In the medication record
    - place your initials on the medication sheet
      - across from the medication administered
      - next to the correct time
      - under the correct date
  - if it is the first time you are administering the medication, for the month, sign your full name and initial the signature list.

  - In the Count Book (if the medication is countable)
    - use the index to locate the correct person, medication and count sheet page number, then,
      - turn to the corresponding count sheet
      - subtract the number of tablets you removed from the package and pay attention to your math; ensuring the number you document in the amount left column is the same as the number of tablets left in the package.

- Secure the medication

- Wash your hands

- Observe the person for the effects of the medication

If you are administering multiple medications due at the same time, to one person, complete Checks 1 through 3 for each medication. All medication due at the same time, for the same person, may be given together and placed in the same medication cup; liquid medication is measured and placed in a separate medication cup.

If you are administering more than one liquid medication, due at the same time, to one person, each liquid medication is measured and placed in a separate medication cup.

Massachusetts | Responsibilities in Action

Medication Administration Process

Prepare

Wash the area and your hands
Look at the medication sheet to identify the medication to administer
Unlock and remove the medication you are administering

Administer

Check 1-verbalize and point to compare the 5 Rights (HCP order and pharmacy label)
Check 2-verbalize and point to compare the 5 Rights (pharmacy label and med sheet)
Prepare the medication
Check 3-verbalize and point to compare the 5 Rights (pharmacy label and med sheet)
Give the med
Look back (silent comparison between pharmacy label and med sheet)

Complete

Document
   1. Medication Record
   2. Count Book, if needed
Secure the medication and wash your hands
Observe

Medication Administration Process

WASH Area & Hands	**LOOK FOR** Medication Record	**UNLOCK** Medication Area	Prepare
1 HCP Order to Pharmacy Label	**2** Pharmacy Label to Medication Sheet	**PREPARE**	Administer
3 Pharmacy Label to Medication Sheet	**GIVE**	**SILENT** Look Back	
DOCUMENT 1. Medication Sheet 2. Count Sheet, if needed	**LOCK** Medication Area	**WASH HANDS** **OBSERVE**	Complete

2020 The Massachusetts Departments of Public Health, Developmental Services, Mental Health, Children and Families and the Rehabilitation Commission

Massachusetts | Responsibilities in Action 138

In addition to hand washing, there may be times when wearing gloves is necessary such as when applying an ointment to a skin rash or when administering a rectal suppository.

To put the gloves on:

- wash your hands as described in the 'Prepare' section of the medication administration process, then

- put on each glove to cover your entire hand and wrist.

To take the gloves off:

- With one gloved hand, take hold of the other glove at the wrist

- Turn the glove inside out as you peel it off your hand

- Roll the removed glove in your hand still wearing a glove

- With your ungloved hand, insert your index finger down the wrist of your still gloved hand pulling the glove down and inside out over the rolled glove

  o At this point both gloves are off with one glove tucked inside the other glove

- Throw away the used gloves into the trash

- Wash your hands

Do not administer medication if

- you cannot read the HCP order
- there is no HCP order
- you cannot read the pharmacy label
- there is no pharmacy label
- you have any concern that the 5 Rights do not agree between the
    - HCP order
    - pharmacy label
    - medication sheet
- a medication seems to be tampered (altered)
- the medication was prepared by someone else
- the person
    - has a serious change
    - has difficulty swallowing
    - refuses to take the medication
- the pharmacy supplied a liquid form of medication, you have been giving the tablet form and there is no change in the HCP order
- the medication was 'pre-poured'

In addition, never use another person's medication to give to someone else for any reason, even if they have the same medication and dose ordered.

Liquid Medication

When the medication is in a liquid form, the identical medication administration process is followed as described earlier. Liquid medications are products you may see labeled as a solution, suspension, syrup or an elixir. Some medications are only available as liquids. Liquid medications must be measured.

Liquid medications are usually measured in milliliters. The abbreviation for milliliter is 'mL'. If abbreviations are used on the pharmacy label read them carefully.

You will notice the label on a liquid medication includes the strength of the medication based on how many milligrams (mg) per milliliters (mL) are measured.

The strength on the Phenytoin label tells you that for every 5mL of liquid measured there is an equivalent of 125mg of the medication.

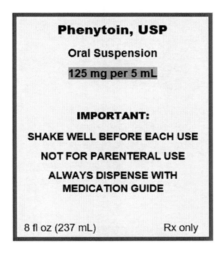

If you measure 10mL, how many milligrams of medication do you have? _____

Remember, whenever a medication has a pharmacy label, the pharmacist will indicate the strength supplied and the amount to administer on the label.

For purposes of this exercise, review the labels and write the strength of each medication.

1. Oral Saline Laxative strength _____ mg per _____ mL

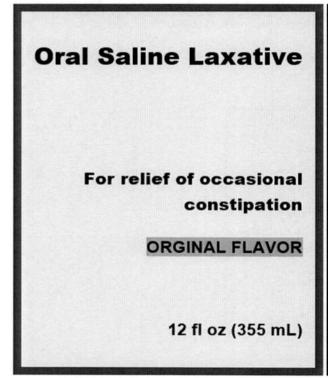

If the dose ordered by the HCP is 2400mg, using the measuring device below, shade in the amount to administer based on the dose ordered and the strength supplied.

Massachusetts | Responsibilities in Action

2. Expectorant Guiafenesin Syrup strength _____ mg per _____ mL

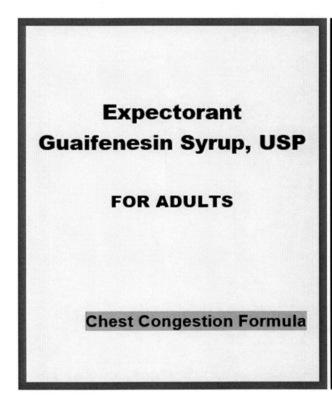
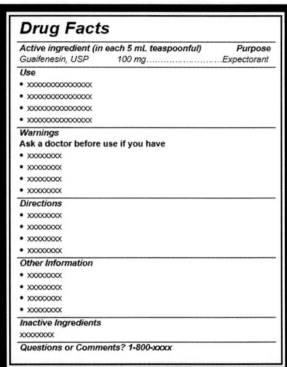

If the dose ordered by the HCP is 200mg, using the measuring device below, shade in the amount to administer based on the dose ordered and the strength supplied.

3. Bismuth Subsalicylate strength _____ mg per _____ mL

If the dose ordered by the HCP is 262mg, using the measuring device below, shade in the amount to administer based on the dose ordered and the strength supplied.

Always use a proper measuring device. Use the device that comes with the medication. If one is not provided, you must ask the pharmacist for an appropriate measuring device. Types of liquid measuring devices include a medication cup, oral syringe, a dropper and dosing spoon.

Some oral liquid measuring devices include a combination of markings (measurements) such as, milliliter (mL), teaspoon, or tablespoon. If you are unsure of which marking to use, contact the MAP Consultant.

If teaspoons are confused with tablespoons, this could result in a three times over- or under-dose. If milliliters are confused with teaspoons, this could result in a five times over- or under-dose.

Medication Cup

Find the marking on the cup that agrees with the amount you need for the dose ordered. When preparing a liquid medication, once you determine the amount of liquid to measure into the medication cup based on the dose ordered, make sure you:

- Shake the medication, if needed
- Remove the cap and place it upside down
    - this will help to keep the medication free of germs
- Place the medication cup on a flat surface, at eye level
    - do not hold it in your hand
- Locate the correct measurement on the medication cup
- Hold the bottle so that your hand covers the pharmacy label
    - this keeps the label from becoming soiled
- Pour slowly
    - if you pour too much, do not pour back into the bottle
    - use a second medication cup to pour into and measure again
    - extra medication must be disposed per MAP Policy
- Wipe the top of the bottle after pouring, if needed
- After use, wash the medication cup if reusing
    - with dish soap and water

Massachusetts | Responsibilities in Action 145

If two liquid medications are due at the same time, each liquid medication is measured using a different medication cup.

Sometimes the amount of liquid medication to be administered is so small; the medication can only be measured accurately using an oral syringe or a dropper or a dosing spoon.

Oral Syringe

Oral syringes come in different sizes. The most common sizes are 1mL, 2.5mL and 5mL syringes, but there are 10mL and larger syringes. Find the measurement on the oral syringe that agrees with the amount you need for the correct dose.

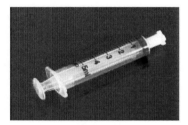

Many times a pharmacy will provide an alternative bottle cap or an adapter that fits on the top of the bottle to allow the liquid to be withdrawn directly from the container with an oral syringe.

When preparing a liquid medication, once you know the amount of liquid to be measured into the oral syringe based on the dose ordered, make sure you:

- Shake the medication, if needed
- Remove the lid and
    - push the adapter firmly into the top of the bottle or
    - screw the alternative cap on the bottle
- Push the tip of the oral syringe into the hole
    - in the adapter or an
    - alternative cap
- Turn the bottle upside down
    - Pull the plunger of the syringe back so that the medicine is drawn from the bottle into the syringe
    - Continue to pull the plunger back to the marking that corresponds to the dose

- If you are unsure about how much medication to draw into the syringe, contact the MAP Consultant
- Remove any large air bubbles from the syringe
  - Air bubbles within an oral syringe can give an inaccurate measurement
  - If there are air bubbles, empty the syringe back into the bottle and try again
- Turn the bottle back the right way up
- Remove the syringe
- After use wash with warm water and dish soap and leave apart to dry

Dropper

A dropper is a glass or plastic tube that is narrow at one end and has a rubber end at the other end that is squeezed in order to measure and sometimes administer medication. Droppers come in different sizes with different markings and are used for different reasons. There are droppers used to administer liquid oral medication, eye droppers and ear droppers. If a dropper comes with the medication, always use the dropper included.

When preparing a liquid medication, once you know the amount of liquid to be measured into the dropper based on the dose ordered, make sure you:

- Hold the dropper upright
  - Do not pull the medication up into the rubber end (bulb) of a dropper or turn the dropper upside down
- Squeeze the bulb of the dropper
  - This will squeeze excess air out of the dropper and prepare the dropper to suck up the medication
- Place the dropper into the bottle
- Slowly let pressure off of the bulb
  - You will see the medication being pulled up into the dropper

- When you get the medication pulled up to the mark of the amount needed
  - Measure at eye level
    - Squeeze the bulb to either remove extra medication or to pull up more medication if needed
- Let go of the rubber end
  - This will cause an air bubble to pop up and look like the medication is off measurement, but you have the correct amount in the dropper

Some droppers are made to be taken apart and cleaned after use. If you are using this type of dropper, remove the bulb from the dropper and wash both pieces with warm water and dish soap, rinse well and let the parts air dry.

Dosing Spoon

Dosing spoons come in different sizes with different markings.

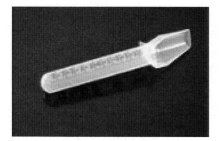

When preparing a liquid medication, once you know the amount of liquid to be measured into the dosing spoon based on the dose ordered, make sure you:

- Hold the dosing spoon upright
- Find the marking for the amount needed based on the dose ordered
- Slowly pour the medication from the bottle into the spoon at eye level
- After use, wash the spoon with warm water and dish soap, rinse and let it air dry

Never measure liquid medications with household utensils or measuring spoons. They are not consistent in their size and will result in either too much or too little medication administered.

Look at the dose ordered by the HCP, the strength of the liquid medication supplied by the pharmacy and fill in the amount to administer you would expect to see printed in the pharmacy label directions.

	Dose	Strength	Amount
1.	150mg	75mg/10mL	
2.	100mg	50mg/6mL	
3.	100mg	50mg/2mL	
4.	150mg	75mg/4mL	
5.	200mg	100mg/5mL	
6.	150mg	50mg/3mL	
7.	100mg	25mg/2mL	
8.	500mg	250mg/10mL	
9.	100mg	100mg/15mL	
10.	500mg	500mg/30mL	
11.	500mg	125mg/5mL	

You are preparing Tanisha's liquid medication. After completing your first two checks in the medication administration process, you are now ready to measure the medication. The amount is listed as 4 mL and to use a special dropper. You cannot locate the dropper. Check what you should do next.

1. ____ Obtain a teaspoon from the kitchen drawer and pour just a little less since a teaspoon is 5mL.

2. ____ Borrow the special dropper that comes with Juanita's liquid medication since it would have 4mL clearly marked for administration.

3. ____ Call the pharmacy and request an appropriate measuring device.

4. ____ Use a medication cup that has markings for 2.5mL and 5 mL and pour just under the 5 mL marking.

Match the following terms with the corresponding letter.

1. ____ Medication cup   A. Must be held upright and at eye level for measuring

2. ____ Oral syringe   B. Squeeze the bulb to draw up medication

3. ____ Dropper   C. Place on a flat surface at eye level

4. ____ Dosing spoon   D. Pull the plunger back to the correct measurement

True (T) or False (F)

1. ____ If a household teaspoon is used as a liquid measuring device this could result in an over- or under-dose.
2. ____ Whether preparing liquids or tablets, the same medication administration process is followed.
3. ____ When pouring liquid medication from a bottle, your hand should cover the label.
4. ____ Two different liquid medications may be measured in the same medication cup.
5. ____ Air bubbles within an oral syringe can give an inaccurate measurement.
6. ____ An oral syringe may be washed and reused for the same person.

How to Document if a Medication is Not Administered

There are times when you may have to document that a medication was not administered, such as when a medication:

- is refused
- order includes parameters of when to hold (not give) a medication
- is held prior to testing
- is not available to administer

Medication Refusals

Sometimes a person may not want to take their medication. This is called a medication refusal. When a person refuses, ask them why. Their answer is important. If the person you are working with does not speak, notice if they keep their lips sealed and turn away from you or seem to frown as they try to swallow the medication before spitting it out, etc.

Your subjective and objective observations are important when reporting the refusal to the prescribing HCP and may result in the HCP changing the current medication order. The HCP may prefer to consult with a Behavior Specialist as well as other team members and develop a plan to manage refusals.

Medication refusals are defined as when the person:

- says 'No'
- spits the medication right back out or never takes the medication from you
- spits the medication out later, even though when you administered it, the person seemed to swallow it
- intentionally vomits the medication within one half hour of taking it

If the person says no or never takes the medication from you, secure it, wait 15-20 minutes and offer the medication again. When offering a second time if the person still refuses, secure it, wait another 15-20 minutes and offer the medication a third time. When offered a third time if the person still refuses the medication, this is considered a final refusal. A person has up to three times to refuse a medication before you are to consider it a final refusal.

All refusals must be reported immediately to the prescribing HCP. It is very important that the prescribing HCP be notified that the person is refusing to take the medication as ordered.

Massachusetts | Responsibilities in Action

The prescribing HCP must be notified every time a person refuses a medication. If the prescribing HCP would prefer to be notified less often than the requirement, a HCP order is required; for example, 'Notify HCP after two refusals within a week'.

When medication is refused, document this on the medication sheet by:

- circling your initials
- writing a medication progress note including
  - the date, time
  - the medication involved
  - why the medication was not administered
  - your observations
  - who was notified
    - the prescribing HCP
    - your Supervisor
      - include first and last names
  - what you were instructed to do
  - your signature

Massachusetts | Responsibilities in Action   152

Documentation example of a refused medication; on the medication sheet and corresponding medication progress note:

Month and Year: February, yr

MEDICATION ADMINISTRATION SHEET

Allergies: none

		Hour	1	2	3	4	5	6	7	8	9	10	11	12	13	14	15	16	17	18	19	20	21	22	23	24	25	26	27	28	29	30	31
Start 8/31/yr	Generic Clonazepam	8am	JS	JS	(JS)																													
	Brand Klonopin																																	
	Strength 1mg Dose 1mg																																	
Stop	Amount 1 tab Route mouth																																	
cont	Frequency twice daily 8am and 4pm	8pm	TM	TM																														

Special instructions:

Reason: seizures

Name   Tanisha Johnson

MEDICATION PROGRESS NOTE

February, yr

Date	Time	Medication	Dose	Given	Not Given	Refused	Other	Reason (for giving/not giving)	Results and/or Response	Staff Signature
2-3-yr 9:15am Tanisha refused her morning Clonazepam 1mg. I attempted to administer it 3 times. Dr. Lee was notified. He recommended to skip this dose and to administer the next dose when it is due. Linda White, supervisor was also notified. Jenna Sherman										

You are responsible for medication administration on March 4, yr. You prepare David's 4pm medication. As you enter the room with his Prilosec, he is pacing back and forth and states, 'I don't want that medication'. You should:

1. ___ Tell David he has to take his medication
2. ___ Dispose of the medication since he doesn't want it
3. ___ Ask David why he doesn't want to take the medication
4. ___ Consider the medication refused

David tells you he doesn't like the purple color of the tablet. You should:

1. ___ Hide the pill in his food so he cannot see the color purple
2. ___ Insist he take the medication because it's ordered by the doctor
3. ___ Leave the pill with David and hope that he will take it
4. ___ Secure the medication, return in 15 minutes and offer it again

Massachusetts | Responsibilities in Action

After 3 attempts, David still refuses the medication. You should first:

1. ___ Notify your Supervisor and coworkers of the refusal
2. ___ Wait one more hour and offer the medication a fourth time
3. ___ Save the medication for the next scheduled administration time
4. ___ Notify Dr. Black of the refusal

Using the medication sheet and corresponding progress note, document the medication refusal.

Month and Year: March, yr   **MEDICATION ADMINISTRATION SHEET**   **Allergies: none**

Start	Generic **Omeprazole**		Hour	1	2	3	4	5	6	7	8	9	10	11	12	13	14	15	16	17	18	19	20	21	22	23	24	25	26	27	28	29	30	31
8/31/yr	Brand **Prilosec**																																	
	Strength **20mg**	Dose **20mg**																																
Stop	Amount **1 tab**	Route **mouth**	4pm	WS	WD	JC																												
Cont.	Frequency **Once daily before supper**																																	

Special instructions: *Reason:* **GERD**

Name David Cook   **MEDICATION PROGRESS NOTE**

Date	Time	Medication	Dose	Given	Not Given	Refused	Other	Reason (for giving/not giving)	Results and/or Response	Staff Signature

Massachusetts | Responsibilities in Action   154

Class Discussion

Scott Green recently began refusing his Zyprexa ordered once a day in the evening. Zyprexa is an antipsychotic medication that Scott's HCP prescribed to help manage schizophrenia. Zyprexa can help calm 'racing thoughts' and when Scott had racing thoughts in the past, he experienced symptoms in a way that he needed to be hospitalized for his safety and the safety of others. He refused three times within the last week and each time staff notified the prescribing HCP of the refusal and the past recent refusals.

1. Why is it important to report each refusal to the prescribing HCP?
   _____
   _____

2. Why is it important to report the previous refusals? _____
   _____
   _____

3. What could occur if the prescribing HCP is not notified of all recent refusals?
   _____
   _____

Scott Green recently refused his medication for management of his schizophrenia. He refused it on Monday, Tuesday and Thursday. You are working on Friday and prepare the medication. Scott refuses the medication even after you attempt to administer it three times.

The most complete information to report to the prescribing HCP is:

1. ___ Scott refused his antipsychotic medication on Friday, even though you attempted to administer it 3 times.
2. ___ Scott refused his antipsychotic medication on Friday and previously on Monday, Tuesday and Thursday.
3. ___ Scott has a history of refusing his medication and refused his antipsychotic medication on Friday; it is his right to refuse medication.

Massachusetts | Responsibilities in Action

Parameters

Parameters are a set of rules that tell you how something should be done. Another word for parameters is guidelines. Specific to medication administration, HCP orders may include parameters that tell you exactly what to do before or after you administer a medication and when to notify the HCP, if needed.

This is an example of a HCP order that includes a parameter telling you when to give a medication:

- give Milk of Magnesia 1200mg by mouth as needed every 3rd evening if no bowel movement

This is an example of a HCP order that includes a parameter telling you when to hold (or not give) a medication:

- take pulse daily before Lisinopril administration, if pulse is less than 60 do not give Lisinopril

These are examples of HCP orders that include a parameter telling you when to notify the HCP:

- if no bowel movement within 24 hours after PRN Milk of Magnesia is administered, notify the HCP
- if pulse is less than 60, hold Lisinopril and notify the HCP
- if complaints of a sore throat, notify the HCP
- if temperature is 100 or greater, notify the HCP

When parameters to hold the medication are met and the medication is not administered, document this on the medication sheet by:

- circling your initials and
- writing a medication progress note including
    - the date, time and
    - the medication involved
    - why the medication was not administered
    - your observations
    - if required, who was notified
        - MAP Consultant
            - typically the HCP
        - your Supervisor
            - include first and last names
        - what you were instructed to do
    - your signature

Massachusetts | Responsibilities in Action

156

The parameters in a person's HCP order (written on the medication sheet next to special instructions) states to hold Zestril if the systolic (top) blood pressure (BP) reading is below 100 and notify the HCP. On March 5th at 8am the BP reading you obtain is 90/50. Use the medication sheet to document the BP reading and the held dose. Use the medication progress note to document what happened and who you notified.

Start	Generic	Hour	1	2	3	4	5	6	7	8	9	10	11	12	13	14	15	16	17	18	19	20	21	22	23	24	25	26	27	28	29	30	31
8/31/yr	Brand **Check blood pressure (BP)**	8am	WS	AS	JC	WS																												
	Strength Dose	BP																																
Stop	Amount Route	S	120	134	130	132																												
Cont.	Frequency **Daily in the morning**	D	64	66	62	60																												

Special instructions: **Hold Zestril if systolic (top) blood pressure (BP) reading is below 100 and notify HCP**   *Reason:*

Start	Generic **Lisinopril**	Hour	1	2	3	4	5	6	7	8	9	10	11	12	13	14	15	16	17	18	19	20	21	22	23	24	25	26	27	28	29	30	31
8/31/yr	Brand **Zestril**	8am	WS	AS	JC	WS																												
	Strength **20mg** Dose **40mg**																																	
Stop	Amount **2 tabs** Route **mouth**																																	
Cont.	Frequency **Daily in the morning**																																	

Special instructions: **Hold Zestril if systolic (top) blood pressure (BP) reading is below 100 and notify HCP**   *Reason:* **high BP**

MEDICATION PROGRESS NOTE

Date	Time	Medication	Dose	Given	Not Given	Refused	Other	Reason (for giving/not giving)	Results and/or Response	Staff Signature

Medication ordered to be held before a medical test

There are some medical tests that require restrictions of food, drink and/or medication prior to testing. A HCP order will specify if medication is to be held before a medical test and whether or not to give the medication after the test is completed or to resume the next regularly scheduled dose as ordered.

When medication is ordered to be held (not administered) prior to a medical test, document this on the medication sheet by:

- circling your initials and
- writing a medication progress note including
    - the date, time and
    - the medication involved
    - why the medication was not administered
        - reference the HCP order to hold the dose of medication prior to testing
    - your signature

The instructions in a person's HCP order state to hold the Omeprazole on March 4, yr at 4pm prior to a scheduled test and to resume the next dose when it is due. Document the held medication dose on the medication sheet and write a medication progress note.

Start	Generic **Omeprazole**		Hour	1	2	3	4	5	6	7	8	9	10	11	12	13	14	15	16	17	18	19	20	21	22	23	24	25	26	27	28	29	30	31
8/31/yr	Brand **Prilosec**																																	
	Strength **20mg**	Dose **20mg**																																
Stop	Amount **1 tab**	Route **mouth**	4pm	WS	WD	JC																												
Cont.	Frequency **Once daily before supper**																																	

Special instructions: *Reason:* **GERD**

MEDICATION PROGRESS NOTE

Date	Time	Medication	Dose	Given	Not Given	Refused	Other	Reason (for giving/not giving)	Results and/or Response	Staff Signature

Massachusetts | Responsibilities in Action

If a medication is not available to administer

At times a medication may not be available to administer even though you have attempted to obtain the medication from the pharmacy such as when

- prior authorization is required from the person's prescription insurance company
  - Follow up by immediately contacting the prescribing HCP and obtain a HCP order about what you are to do until the medication can be obtained
- the medication is 'too soon to refill'
  - Follow up by contacting the pharmacist and asking when the medication will be available and what you are to do until the medication is obtained
- no refills remain on the prescription
  - Follow up by immediately contacting the prescribing HCP and request a new prescription be sent to the pharmacy
    - follow up with the pharmacy to ensure the prescription is received
    - confirm a date and a time the medication will be obtained
      - if you cannot obtain the medication for the dose that is due obtain a HCP order about what you should do

Prior authorization is when the HCP must obtain approval from the person's health insurance company to prescribe a specific medication for that person.

When medication is not available to be administered, document this on the medication sheet by:

- circling your initials and
- writing a medication progress note including
  - the date, time and
  - the medication involved
  - why the medication was not administered
  - what you have done to obtain the medication
  - your observations
  - who was notified
    - Pharmacist and/or HCP
    - your Supervisor
      - include first and last names
  - what you were instructed to do
  - your signature

There is no Prilosec available for you to administer at 4pm on March 4th, yr. You call and speak to Forrest Greenleaf the pharmacist at Greenleaf Pharmacy. You were told the medication will be delivered by 7:30pm. You then ask the pharmacist what to do about the 4pm dose that will be missed. The pharmacist's recommendation is to omit the 4pm dose on March 4th, yr and to give the next regularly scheduled dose when due. Document the missed dose on the medication sheet and write a medication progress note.

Start	Generic **Omeprazole**			Hour	1	2	3	4	5	6	7	8	9	10	11	12	13	14	15	16	17	18	19	20	21	22	23	24	25	26	27	28	29	30	31
8/31/yr	Brand **Prilosec**																																	
	Strength **20mg**	Dose **20mg**																																
Stop	Amount **1 tab**	Route **mouth**		4pm	WS	WD	JC																											
Cont.	Frequency **Once daily before supper**																																	

Special instructions: *Reason:* **GERD**

MEDICATION PROGRESS NOTE

Date	Time	Medication	Dose	Given	Not Given	Refused	Other	Reason (for giving/not giving)	Results and/or Response	Staff Signature

When a medication is not available and as a result is omitted (not given), it is a medication occurrence; requiring you to contact a MAP Consultant immediately and complete a medication occurrence report form, if applicable.

Massachusetts | Responsibilities in Action

Let's Review

- Some medications are administered on a continuous basis
- Some medications are administered on a PRN, as needed basis
    - PRN medication orders must have
        - target signs and symptoms
        - a specific reason for use
        - parameters or instructions
            - including what to do if the medication is given and does not work
- There are 5 Rights of Medication Administration
    - Person
    - Medication
    - Dose
    - Time
    - Route
- The 5 Rights must agree between the
    - HCP order
    - Pharmacy label
    - Medication sheet
- The 5 Rights must be checked 3 times before any medication is administered
    - Check 1-HCP order and pharmacy label
    - Check 2-Pharmacy label and medication sheet
    - Check 3-Pharmacy label and medication sheet
- Liquid medication strength will usually have a 'mg' per 'mL'
- Liquid measuring devices must always be used to prepare liquid medication
- There are many different routes that medications can be administered
    - Routes other than oral require additional training
- A HCP order is required to change the form of a medication (such as crushing)
- If a person refuses their medication try to determine why
- Offer the medication 3 times before considering the medication refused
- Documentation of a medication not administered includes
    - Your initials circled on the medication sheet
    - A progress note indicating
        - why the medication was not administered
        - recommendations given
        - who was notified (HCP and Supervisor)

Massachusetts | Responsibilities in Action   161

Unit 8

Chain of Custody

Responsibilities you will learn

- What the 'Chain of Custody' means
- Why the Chain of Custody is necessary
- What can happen if the Chain of Custody is broken
- Your role in the Chain of Custody

Access to the medication storage area must be limited to staff assigned to administer medication. Only MAP Certified staff may know the combination to access the medication storage keys. Once you are assigned medication administration duties you are responsible for the inventory (supply) of medication during your assigned shift.

When countable controlled medications are part of the inventory, every time the medication storage keys change hands conduct a two person, 'Shoulder to Shoulder', count of the medication with the incoming and outgoing responsible staff.

Once you have conducted the count and have accepted the keys, only you should have access to the medication storage area. The medication keys are kept with you as long as you are in the program. At the end of your shift, you will conduct a two person count with the incoming staff that will be responsible for the medication before handing the keys over.

If the Certified staff assigned to administer medication and/or maintain medication security changes during a shift and the keys are passed, a count must be completed at that time.

If there will be no Certified staff in the program during the next shift, the keys must be kept locked in the program. Medication storage keys are typically secured in a combination locked box. A count must be completed before placing the keys into the locked box and/or after removing the keys from the locked box.

The Chain of Custody is an unbroken documentation trail of accountability that ensures the physical security of medication. The Chain of Custody tracks every tablet, capsule, mL, etc. of medication, from the time it is requested from the pharmacy, either as a new medication or a medication refill, until the time it no longer exists in the program (administered, disposed, transferred etc.).

The Chain of Custody ensures the integrity of the medication is not compromised and all medication is accounted for. Maintaining the Chain of Custody minimizes the opportunity for medication to be diverted (stolen).

There are many documents and methods used to track medications. Those include:

- A Medication Ordering and Receiving Log
  - Documentation of medication that is ordered by a program and when it is received from the pharmacy.

- Pharmacy receipts
  - Documentation from the pharmacy of all medication dispensed to a program; whether delivered to the program or picked up from the pharmacy by Certified staff.

- Count Book
  - Documentation of countable medication that is added into the Count Book and/or subtracted from a Count Book.

- Medication sheet
  - Documentation of medication that is administered and (if) not administered.

- Medication release documents (Transfer or LOA form)
  - Documentation of medication that is moved from one location to another location.

- Disposal Record
  - Documentation of medication that is disposed.

- Blister Pack Monitoring
  - A medication tracking mechanism. Although not a MAP requirement, if used at your program, documentation is completed by staff on the back of the blister pack, each time a tablet or capsule is removed from the package.

Ask your Supervisor if blister pack monitoring is required at your work location.

Medication Ordering and Receiving Log

All programs must maintain a record of when a prescription is requested to be filled by the pharmacy with the corresponding quantity of medication received. This process is typically documented using a Medication Ordering and Receiving Log. You must document in the Medication Ordering and Receiving Log each time you:

- request a medication refill from the pharmacy, document the
  - person's name
  - name of medication and strength
  - quantity (total number of tablets, capsules, mL, etc. requested)
  - HCP's name
  - your signature and the date the medication refill was requested
- receive a medication refill from the pharmacy, document the
  - prescription (Rx) number
  - strength of medication received
    - double check that the strength ordered is the same as the strength received
  - quantity (total number of tablets, capsules, mL, etc. received)
  - remaining refills
    - if "0", contact the HCP to request another prescription be sent to the pharmacy
  - your signature and the date the medication refill was received

Sample Medication Ordering and Receiving Log

Provider   **Program Address**   **Pharmacy**

Name	Medication	Strength Ordered	Quantity Ordered	Health Care Provider	Ordered by- Signature/Date	Rx#	Strength Received	Quantity Received	Remaining Refills	Received by- Signature/Date

You have received a delivery of medication from the pharmacy. As you document that the medication is received onto the Medication Ordering and Receiving Log you notice that one of the medications received has "0" refills left.

What should you do next? _____

Pharmacy Receipts

The pharmacy will provide a receipt for every medication dispensed. The pharmacy receipt will typically include the:

- person's name
- medication name
- strength of medication
- total number of tablets, capsules or mL dispensed
- Rx (prescription) number

When medication is received from the pharmacy you must compare the:

- medication received from the pharmacy to the pharmacy receipt
  - ensuring you received what the pharmacy documented they sent
- Medication Ordering and Receiving Log to the medication obtained
  - ensuring you received what was ordered by your program

The pharmacy manifest (receipt of medication dispensed) must be kept at the program for a minimum of 90 days as a way to track medication coming into the program.

If the pharmacy manifest of medication dispensed is used as documentation for the program's receiving system, it must be maintained indefinitely.

Ask your Supervisor if the pharmacy where you work supplies automatic refills or online orders. If the answer is yes, ask what system is used to cross check the medication you are expecting to receive to what the pharmacy delivers.

Countable Controlled Substance Book

The Countable Controlled Substance Book is typically known as the Count Book. All countable controlled (schedule II-V) medication must be documented and tracked in a Count Book. There are many requirements surrounding countable medication because these medications may be stolen and abused.

The Count Book must have a binding with no loose pages. The binding is the adhesive on the edge of the book that holds the pages together and protects them. The book must be preprinted with consecutively numbered pages.

Typically a Count Book will have a page in the front, sometimes with lines that include an area to write in the program address and the book number. If there are no spaces labeled as such, the information may be written on a blank page in the front of the Count Book.

Count Books are consecutively numbered historically for the site, i.e. Count Book 1, Count Book 2, Count Book 3, etc.

A Count Book has 3 basic sections, including the

- Index
- Count Sheets
- Count Signature Sheets

Index

The beginning of the Count Book contains the index. The index will identify the

- name of each person prescribed a countable medication
- medication name and strength
- count sheet page number of the countable medication
- signature space if the medication is removed from count

  o only a supervisor may remove a medication from count including but not limited to, any of the following reasons:

    ▪ the medication was discontinued and disposed
    ▪ the medication was disposed after a person passed
    ▪ the person moved and medication was transferred to a new home
      - the 'amount left column' of the corresponding count sheet page in any of the above examples will be marked as '0', since that medication is physically no longer in the program to count

Index

Name	Medication and Strength	Page Number				Person responsible for removing medication from count
David Cook	Phenobarbital 32.4mg	1	2			
Tanisha Johnson	Clonazepam 1mg	3				
Tanisha Johnson	Phenobarbital 32.4mg	4				
Ellen Tracey	Lorazepam 0.5mg	5				
Juanita Gomez	Tramadol 50mg	6				
David Cook	Tramadol 25mg	7				

Massachusetts | Responsibilities in Action

A Count Book index also identifies the count sheet pages that are currently in use. The index must be updated when transferring from an old count sheet page to a new count sheet page. As the index is updated, the preceding page number is not crossed out. A 'Shoulder to Shoulder' count of all medication is conducted using the index as a guide.

Looking at the sample index below, you know that
- Sarah Brown's phenobarbital is no longer in the double locked area to count because Linda White, the supervisor, signed as removing it from count. If the medication was discontinued, it would have remained on count and double locked until disposed. Only after its disposal would a supervisor sign as 'Person Responsible for Removing Medication from Count'. If you turned to the corresponding count sheet page 7, the 'amount left' column would have a '0' as there is no longer medication physically present to count.

- Mike Stone has Ativan 1mg tablets to be counted on page 5 (because page 2 became full.)

- When the four boxes next to Joseph Smith's Ativan were full, a supervisor wrote 'see below' with their initials to indicate the Ativan was started on a new row in the index. Joseph Smith's Ativan is currently found on count sheet page 11.

- William Mitchell has Percocet to be counted on count sheet page 8.

According to the index below, there are three count sheet pages currently in use, count sheet page numbers 5, 8 and 11.

Index

Name	Medication and Strength	Page Number				Person responsible for removing medication from count
Sarah Brown	Phenobarbital 97.2mg	1	4	7		*Linda White*
Mike Stone	Ativan 1mg	2	5			
Joseph Smith	Ativan 0.5mg	3	6	9	10	*See below LW*
William Mitchell	Percocet 5mg/325mg	8				
Joseph Smith	Ativan 0.5mg	11				

Count Sheets

When a new medication is added into the count or the balance of medication is transferred from a completed count sheet page to a new count sheet page, the heading of the new count sheet page must be completed. The heading of each count sheet must be completed with the information from the pharmacy label, including the

- person's name
- medication name
- strength of medication
- directions to administer the medication
- HCP's name
- pharmacy name
- prescription (Rx) number
- prescription date

The first line of the count sheet must indicate the

- date and time
  - amount of medication received from the pharmacy and added into the count, or
  - amount of medication transferred from a completed count sheet page to a new count sheet page
- signatures of the two Certified staff verifying the amount of new medication added into the count or the amount of medication transferred to the new page

The count sheet tracks the amount of each countable medication when

- added as
  - a new medication
  - a medication refill
  - transferred from a previous page
  - received from another program
  - received from the pharmacy after repackaging and/or relabeling

- subtracted as
  - administered, including the
    - date and time
    - route by which the medication was administered
    - amount on hand (the amount you started with)
    - amount used

Massachusetts | Responsibilities in Action 169

- - amount remaining (the amount you are left with after subtracting what you removed from the package)
    - your signature
  - packaged
    - the total amount of tablets packaged into a pill organizer by a person learning to self-administer
  - transferred
    - to another program, such as the day program
    - on a LOA
    - to the pharmacy for repackaging or relabeling
  - disposed
    - if the medication is
      - refused
      - expired
      - discontinued
      - dropped on floor, etc.

Each tablet, capsule or mL of medication must be accounted for.

The amount used column must be documented in word form, not the numerical form. For example, 'one' must be written and not documented as the number '1'. This will help prevent someone from altering your documentation.

1|Page

Name: David Cook

Doctor: Dr. Black

Pharmacy: Greenleaf

Medication and Strength: Phenobarbital 32.4mg

Directions: Take 3 tablets by mouth once daily in evening

__X__ Original Entry or

_____Transferred from page___

Prescription Number: N671

Prescription Date: Feb. 17, yr

Date	Time	Route	Amount on Hand	Amount Used	Amount Left	Signature
2/17/yr	9am	Received 42 from Pharmacy			42	Linda White/Sam Dowd
2/17/yr	8pm	Mouth	42	Three	39	Jenna Sherman
2/18/yr	8pm	Mouth	39	Three	36	Jenna Sherman
2/19/yr	8pm	Mouth	36	Three	33	Amanda Smith
2/20/yr	8pm	Mouth	33	Three	30	Amanda Smith
2/21/yr	8pm	Mouth	30	Three	27	Amanda Smith
2/22/yr	8pm	Mouth	27	Three	24	Jenna Sherman
2/23/yr	8pm	Mouth	24	Three	21	Jenna Sherman
2/24/yr	8pm	Mouth	21	Three	18	Amanda Smith
2/25/yr	8pm	Mouth	18	Three	15	Amanda Smith
2/26/yr	8pm	Mouth	15	Three	12	Amanda Smith
2/27/yr	8pm	Mouth	12	Three	9	Jenna Sherman
2/28/yr	8pm	Mouth	9	Three	6	Jenna Sherman
3/1/yr	8pm	Mouth	6	Three	3	Amanda Smith
3/2/yr	8pm	Mouth	3	Three	0	Amanda Smith

Amount left __0__ transferred to page __2__

Signature _____ Amanda Smith

Signature _____ Jenna Sherman

2020 The Massachusetts Departments of Public Health, Developmental Services, Mental Health, Children and Families and the Rehabilitation Commission

Massachusetts | Responsibilities in Action

Count Signature Sheets

The last section of the Count Book contains the count signature sheets. Countable controlled medication must be counted

- with two Certified staff
- every time the medication storage keys change hands
  - including, when placing the medication storage keys into or removing them from the combination lock box
    - This can happen when
      - there is no staff coming on duty as you are leaving or
      - there is no staff present when you arrive

Count Signature Sheet

Date	Time	Count correct yes/no	Incoming Staff	Outgoing Staff
3/1/yr	3:10pm	Yes	Amanda Smith	Sam Dowd
3/1/yr	11:06pm	Yes	Jenna Sherman	Amanda Smith
3/2/yr	8:56am	Yes	single person count	Jenna Sherman[*]
3/2/yr	3:04pm	Yes	Sam Dowd	Linda White (witness)[**]
3/2/yr	11:17pm	Yes	Amanda Smith	Sam Dowd

[*] On 3-2-yr at 8:56am, Jenna Sherman was the only MAP Certified staff on duty. When it was time for her to leave, there was no MAP Certified staff coming on duty. Jenna conducted a single person count before securing the medication storage keys.

[**] On 3-2-yr at 3:04pm, a two-person count was conducted by Sam Dowd and Linda White. Sam was assigned medication administration duties for the shift. When documenting, Linda included the word 'witness' next to her signature because she and Sam were working the same shift. Outgoing staff had left earlier that morning.

'Shoulder to Shoulder' Count Procedure

When conducting a two-person count of the countable controlled medication follow the 'Shoulder to Shoulder' count procedure:

- The outgoing staff (giving up the keys) holds the Count Book and leads the count.
  - Using the index as their guide, the outgoing staff reads the information of the first medication to be counted including the person's name, medication name and strength, and then turns to the appropriate count sheet page.

- The incoming staff (receiving the keys) locates the corresponding tamper resistant pack of medication.
  - The incoming staff then reads the label information aloud; the person's name, medication name, strength and directions for use. Then counts and states the number of pills, syringes, etc. seen in the package.

- The outgoing staff (giving up the keys) verifies that the directions listed on the count page is accurate and that the number of pills, syringes etc. in the 'amount left' column is the same as the number as counted by the incoming staff.

- Both staff look at and verify the number of pills, syringes etc. remaining in the tamper resistant package and in the 'amount left' column are the same.

- Both staff inspect the integrity of the package to ensure there has been no tampering.

- This process is completed for each countable medication.

- After all countable medications have been counted, both staff must sign the count signature sheet documenting that the count was conducted and all countable medication is accounted for. When documenting the time the count is completed, look at a clock and document the exact time to the minute. The medication storage keys are now transferred to the incoming staff.

Massachusetts | Responsibilities in Action 173

2020 The Massachusetts Departments of Public Health, Developmental Services, Mental Health, Children and Families and the Rehabilitation Commission

Countable medications must be counted each time the medication storage keys change hands, including when the storage keys are placed into or removed from a lock box. The person assigned medication administration duties must carry the medication storage keys for the shift.

All counts must be conducted by two Certified and/or licensed staff, unless the following conditions are met, in which case, the required count may be conducted by a single Certified and/or licensed staff:

- The required 2 person count has been conducted within the previous 24 hours and
- A second Certified/licensed staff person is not scheduled to be in the program when the responsibility of the control of the medication key needs to be passed.

At the first opportunity, and no later than 24 hours after the last two-person count was conducted, a required two-person count must be conducted.

True (T) or False (F)

1. __ When conducting a two-person medication count, it is acceptable for one staff to conduct the count and then have a second staff verify the count at a later time.
2. __ All countable medications must be counted every time the medication storage keys change hands.
3. __ After counting the medications and accepting the medication storage keys, you are accepting responsibility for the security of the medication.
4. __ The medication storage keys are carried by the Certified staff assigned medication administration duties for the shift.
5. __ Maintaining the Chain of Custody makes it harder for medication to be stolen

Review the scenario and select the best action.

You arrive at work and are assigned medication administration duties for the shift. A 'Shoulder to Shoulder' count is completed, the medication storage keys are handed to you and you have accepted responsibility for the medication. During your shift, another Certified staff asks for the medication storage keys to obtain the drug reference book from the medication storage area. You must:

1. __ Give the keys to the Certified staff with instructions to return them as soon as they have what they need.
2. __ Unlock the medication storage area for the Certified staff and instruct them to lock it back up when they are done.
3. __ Unlock the medication storage area, obtain the drug reference book for the Certified staff and relock.

Mark yes (Y) or no (N) if you may give the medication keys to:
1. __ The VNA nurse who needs to access the insulin stored in the medication area
2. __ Administrator or supervisor that is not MAP Certified requesting to do an audit
3. __ Maintenance personnel for needed repairs to the medication closet

Answer the following questions:
1. What happens to the 'Chain of Custody' if unauthorized staff have access to the medication storage area? _____

2. When and to who are you allowed to give the medication storage keys?
_____
_____

You are one of two Certified staff conducting a 'Shoulder to Shoulder' count. Review count sheet page 9 below and the corresponding blister pack (see next page). Is the count correct? _____

9| P a g e

Name: Scott Green

Doctor: Dr. S. Pratt

Pharmacy: Greenleaf

Medication and Strength: Zolpidem 5mg

__X_ Original Entry or

____Transferred from page__

Prescription Number: N588

Prescription Date: Mar. 3, yr

Directions: Take 1 tablet by mouth once daily PRN at bedtime per Scott's request for difficulty sleeping

Date	Time	Route	Amount on Hand	Amount Used	Amount Left	Signature
3/3/yr	9am	Received 30 from pharmacy			30	Linda White/Sam Dowd
3/3/yr	9pm	mouth	30	One	29	Jenna Sherman
3/4/yr	9pm	mouth	29	One	28	Jenna Sherman
3/8/yr	9:30pm	mouth	28	One	27	Amanda Smith
3/10/yr	9pm	mouth	27	One	26	Amanda Smith
3/11/yr	9:15pm	mouth	26	One	25	Jenna Sherman
3/13/yr	9pm	mouth	25	One	24	Jenna Sherman
3/14/yr	10pm	mouth	24	One	23	Jenna Sherman
3/18/yr	10pm	mouth	23	One	22	Amanda Smith
3/22/yr	9:30pm	mouth	22	One	21	Amanda Smith

Massachusetts | Responsibilities in Action

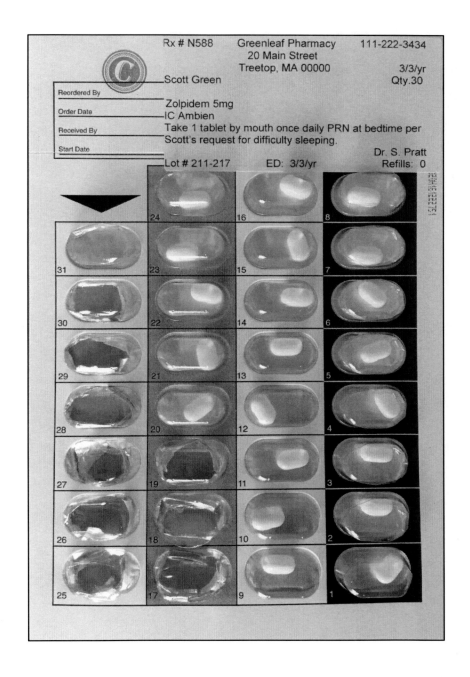

If the tablets in a blister package are accidentally removed out of order, you cannot rely on the numbered blisters; instead you must count each tablet.

Massachusetts | Responsibilities in Action 177

When and Why Two Signatures are Required in the Count Book

Two Certified and/or licensed staff signatures are required in the Count Book when

- adding a newly prescribed medication into the count
  - Why?
    - To verify the total amount of new medication received from the pharmacy is correct, is added to the count and is not stolen.

- adding a medication refill from the pharmacy into the count
  - Why?
    - To verify the total amount of medication received from the pharmacy is correct, is added to the count and is not stolen.

- disposing medication
  - Why?
    - To verify the total amount of medication to be disposed is rendered useless and cannot be used or stolen.

- a count sheet page is transferred, including both the bottom of the completed page and the top of the newly transferred page
  - Why?
    - To verify the amount (number of tabs, caps, mL's etc.) of medication at the bottom of the completed page is the same as the amount of medication at the top of the new page and has not been changed so that the medication can be stolen.

- the medications are counted each time the medication storage keys change hands
  - Why?
    - To verify all medication is secure, accounted for and is not stolen.

8| P a g e

Name: Tanisha Johnson
Doctor: Dr. C. Lee
Pharmacy: Greenleaf
Medication and Strength: Phenobarbital 32.4mg
Directions: Take 2 tablets by mouth once daily in evening

___ Original Entry or
X__ Transferred from page__4__
Prescription Number: N347
Prescription Date: Mar. 3, yr

Date	Time	Route	Amount on Hand	Amount Used	Amount Left	Signature
3/17/yr	9pm		Page Transfer*		32	Jenna Sherman/Amanda Smith
3/18/yr	8pm	Mouth	32	Two	30	Jenna Sherman
3/19/yr	8pm	Mouth	30	Two	28	Jenna Sherman
3/20/yr	8pm	Mouth	28	Two	26	Amanda Smith
3/21/yr	8pm	Mouth	26	Two	24	Amanda Smith
3/22/yr	8pm	Mouth	24	Two	22	Amanda Smith
3/23/yr	8pm	Mouth	22	Two	20	Jenna Sherman
3/24/yr	8pm	Mouth	20	Two	18	Jenna Sherman
3/25/yr	8pm	Mouth	18	Two	16	Amanda Smith
3/26/yr	8pm	Mouth	16	Two	14	Amanda Smith
3/26/yr	9pm		Received 60 from pharmacy**		74	Jenna Sherman/Amanda Smith
3/27/yr	8pm	Mouth	74	Two	72	Amanda Smith

*The 3/17/yr 9:00pm entry is an example of a count sheet page transfer. If you looked back at count sheet page 4 at the bottom, you would see 32 in the amount left column and the signatures of Jenna Sherman and Amanda Smith.

**The 3/26/yr 9:00pm entry is an example of adding a medication refill into count when two MAP Certified staff are working at the same time when a pharmacy delivery arrives.

Massachusetts | Responsibilities in Action

2020 The Massachusetts Departments of Public Health, Developmental Services, Mental Health, Children and Families and the Rehabilitation Commission

Medication Sheets

Medication sheets are tracking forms that are part of the Chain of Custody. All HCP medication orders must be transcribed onto a medication sheet. After a medication is administered you write your initials in the medication box on the medication sheet documenting you have administered the medication.

Your initials in a medication box means that you administered the medication at the program. If the medication was not administered at the program because the person was at another location, an acceptable code is used.

Acceptable Codes on a Medication Sheet

- A - **a**bsent from site (Medication was not administered due to unauthorized reasons beyond staff's control as the person left the program without agreement or supervision or did not return as planned without agreement or supervision during medication administration time.)
- DP - **d**ay **p**rogram/day habilitation (Person's medication responsibilities transferred to a day program or a day habilitation program)
- H - **h**ospital, nursing home, rehab center, respite (Person's medication responsibilities transferred to a hospital, nursing home, rehabilitation center, respite, etc.)
- LOA - **l**eave **o**f **a**bsence (Medication was transferred to family/guardian/responsible party for administration while on leave of absence)
- NSS - **n**o **s**econd **s**taff (Specific to medication that requires dose verification prior to administration by a second staff such as, warfarin sodium, indicates there is no second staff available.)
- OSA - **o**ff-**s**ite **a**dministration (Medication is administered by Certified staff at an off-site location, such as the movies, a community outing, etc.)
- P - **p**ackaged (Person packed their medication under staff supervision. Code is used when a person is learning to self-administer their medication)
- S - **s**chool (Person's medication responsibilities transferred to a school or after school program)
- V - **v**acation (Medication to be administered by Certified staff when the staff accompanies a person on a planned vacation)
- W - **w**ork (Medication to be administered by Certified staff at a person's work location)

Massachusetts | Responsibilities in Action

Based on each scenario, fill in the acceptable code that you would use on the medication sheet.

You are a day program staff:

1. _____ A person did not attend day program because they are on vacation.
2. _____ You will be administering a medication to a person during their work hours.

You are a residential program staff:

1. _____ You have medication administration duties while a person is at the beach for the day.
2. _____ You have medication administration duties while a person is at day program
3. _____ You have medication administration duties while a person is at their family's home over the weekend.
4. _____ You have medication administration duties, a person is not in their home during medication administration time because the person left the program without supervision.
5. _____ You have medication administration duties while one person is away in Florida for the week with another Certified staff.
6. _____ You have medication administration duties while a person is at work.

If the person is at the program but the medication is not administered, document this on the medication sheet by

- circling your initials and
  - writing a progress note explaining
    - why the medication was not administered and
    - who was notified

Massachusetts | Responsibilities in Action   181

Documentation example of a medication missed (omitted); on the medication sheet and corresponding medication progress note:

Month and Year: June, yr **MEDICATION ADMINISTRATION SHEET** **Allergies: Bactrim**

Start 2/1/yr	Generic Phenytoin		Hour	1	2	3	4	5	6	7	8	9	10	11	12	13	14	15	16	17	18	19	20	21	22	23	24	25	26	27	28	29	30	31
	Brand Dilantin		8am	JS	JS	JS	JS	JS	AS	AS	AS	AS	JS	JS	JS	JS	JS	AS	AS	AS	AS	JS	JS	JS	JS	(JS)								
	Strength 100mg	Dose 200mg																																
Stop	Amount 2 tabs	Route mouth																																
cont.	Frequency twice daily		8pm	TM	TM	SD	SD	SD	SD	SD	TM	TM	TM	TM	SD	SD	SD	SD	SD	TM	TM	TM	TM	SD	SD									

Special instructions: *Reason: seizures*

Name Juanita Gomez **MEDICATION PROGRESS NOTE**

Date	Time	Medication	Dose	Given	Not Given	Refused	Other	Reason (for giving/not giving)	Results and/or Response	Staff Signature
6-23-yr 9:30am Juanita's morning dose of Phenytoin 200mg was omitted. The refill was not included in this morning's delivery. The pharmacy was contacted and said the medication will be delivered by 2pm today. I spoke to the pharmacist, Forrest Greenleaf who told me to skip this morning's dose and give the 8pm dose as ordered. He also recommended notifying the neurologist. I notified Dr. Jones who had no further recommendations. I also reported the information to Linda White, Supervisor. Jenna Sherman										

When a medication is not available and as a result is omitted (not given), it is a medication occurrence requiring you to contact a MAP Consultant immediately and complete a medication occurrence report form.

Medication Release Documents

A medication release document is used to track medication. When medication is moved from one location to another location, such as from a residential program to

- the day program/day habilitation
- family for a LOA
- a different residential program
- the pharmacy for repackaging or re-labeling
- the hospital because a specific medication prescribed for the person is not supplied by the hospital's pharmacy

a dated medication release document (transfer or LOA form) must be completed.

The medication release document must include:

- The name of the person whose medication is being moved
- Where the medication is being transferred from
- Where the medication is being transferred to
- Medication name and strength
- Total amount of medication (tablets, capsules, mL, etc.) transferred
- Signature of person transferring medication
- Signature of person receiving medication

Sample Medication Transfer Form

I, _____, am transferring the following medication

For (Name), _____

From _____

To _____

Date _____

Medication	Strength	Quantity

Signature of staff receiving medications _____ Date _____

Signature of staff transferring medications _____ Date _____

Medications are transported only by MAP Certified or licensed staff for the people residing at their work location and only during work hours. MAP Certified staff may not transport medications for persons living outside of the staff's work location or on the staff's own time.

Medication Administration at Locations other than the Residential Program

Whenever possible schedule medication to be administered in the residential program. However, if a person requires medication at locations other than the residential program, it may be administered.

Medication administration at locations other than the residential program may include:

- Day Program
- Off-Site Medication Administration
- Leave of Absence
- Certified/Licensed Staffed Vacation

Day Program Medication and Residential Program Staff Responsibilities

If a person will routinely be receiving medications at more than one location, such as the day program, ask the pharmacy to 'split-package' or divide the medication into two containers, one for the residential program and one for the day program.

For example, if Juanita attends day program five days a week, the pharmacy will prepare and package her day program medication separately from medication she receives at her residential program. If Juanita's monthly supply of medication is delivered in full to the residential program,

- before you send it to the day program,
  - document the medication as received into the residential program's Medication Ordering and Receiving Log
    - if the medication is a countable medication, add it to the Count Book
    - complete a release form for the split-packaged day program medication including
      - name of person
      - medication name and strength
      - amount of tablets, capsules or mL released
        - if the medication is a countable medication, it must be subtracted from the residential program's Count Book
      - address the medication is being released from
      - address the medication is being released to
      - your signature, as the person releasing the medication
      - date

- at the day program
  - obtain signature and date, of person accepting the medication
    - if the medication is a countable medication, day program staff must add it to the Count Book
    - make a copy of the signed and dated transfer form
      - the residential program needs a copy as documentation of medication released and
      - the day program needs a copy as documentation of medication received

Day program staff typically receives their supply of medication from residential program staff. In this instance, a day program will not be able to meet the MAP requirement of having 90 days' worth of pharmacy receipts in the program; instead, a day program will have transfer forms which are kept indefinitely.

It is the residential program staff's responsibility to ensure the day program staff has everything that is required for medication administration:

- a copy of the HCP order and
- pharmacy labeled split-packaged medication

Communication between residential program staff and day program staff is essential for safe medication administration.

Class Discussion

Juanita has a medication ordered four times daily, scheduled for 8am, 12pm, 4pm and 8pm; the 12pm dose is administered at the day program 5 days a week. At Juanita's last HCP visit Dr. Jones discontinued the medication. The residential staff discontinued the order on the medication sheet, posted and verified the HCP order and disposed of the discontinued medication, per agency policy. However, no one notified the day program. What do you think happened? What should have happened?

Ask your supervisor what the communication system is between the day program and your work location.

Day Program Staff Responsibilities

Day programs must have a system in place to ensure a complete set of current HCP orders are received from the residential program for each person; this includes PRN medication orders that may be needed during day program hours.

Day program staff must verify that the amount of medication received from residential program staff is adequate and is not too much or too little.

Only medications scheduled during day program hours and PRN medications that may be needed during day program hours are transcribed onto the medication sheet.

Residential program staff informs day program staff that David Cook has a new order for Amoxicillin 500mg every 8 hours for 10 days by mouth because he has bronchitis. The times chosen by residential program staff were 6am-2pm-10pm. His first dose was at 10pm on May 2, yr.

After resting at home for several days, David has received medical clearance to return to the day program on Monday, May 8, yr.

Using the copy of the HCP order and the pharmacy labeled medication package (see following two pages) supplied by residential program staff, day program staff will transcribe the order onto a medication sheet.

HEALTH CARE PROVIDER ORDER

Name: David Cook	**Date:** May 2, yr
Health Care Provider: Dr. Black	**Allergies:** No Known Allergies
Reason for Visit: David has had a cough since yesterday. He is complaining of a sore throat and says he 'feels tired'. His temperature was 100 at 9am today.	
Current Medications: See attached medication list.	
Staff Signature: Sam Dowd	**Date:** May 2, yr
Health Care Provider Findings: Bronchitis	
Medication/Treatment Orders: Amoxicillin 500mg every 8 hours for 10 days by mouth	
Instructions:	
Follow-up visit:	**Lab work or Tests:**
Signature: *Richard Black, MD*	**Date:** May 2, yr

Posted by: **Sam Dowd** Date: 5/2/yr Time: 1:15pm Verified by: *Linda White* Date: 5/2/yr Time: 2pm
Posted by: *Tom Cash* Date: 5/8/yr Time: 8:10am Verified by: *Sara Green* Date: 5/8/yr Time: 9am

After transcribing, day program staff must post and verify the HCP order under the post and verify section that was completed by residential program staff.

Rx #210	Greenleaf Pharmacy	111-222-3443
	20 Main Street	
	Treetop, MA 00000	5/2/yr
David Cook		
Amoxicillin 500mg		Qty. 30
IC Amoxil		
Take 1 tablet by mouth every 8 hours for 10 days		
		Dr. Black
Lot# 436	ED: 5/2/yr	Refills: 0

At the day program, when transcribing you must use and copy all of the specific times chosen by residential staff. This includes the times in which the medication is administered at the residential program.

Only the medication boxes in which medication will be administered at the day program are left open for staff initials after medication administration.

All medication boxes of times and or days of the week (Saturday, Sunday, holidays, etc.) that do not apply to day program hours are marked with an 'X' in the medication box.

Month and Year: May, yr | **MEDICATION ADMINISTRATION SHEET** | **Allergies: none**

Start 5/2/yr	Generic Amoxicillin			Hour	1	2	3	4	5	6	7	8	9	10	11	12	13	14	15	16	17	18	19	20	21	22	23	24	25	26	27	28	29	30	31
	Brand Amoxil			6am	X	X	X	X	X	X	X	X	X	X	X	X	X	X	X	X	X	X	X	X	X	X	X	X	X	X	X	X	X	X	X
	Strength 500mg	Dose 500mg																																
Stop	Amount 1 tab	Route mouth		2pm	X	X	X	X	X	X	X					X	X	X	X	X	X	X	X	X	X	X	X	X	X	X	X	X	X	X	X
5/12/yr	Frequency Every 8 hours for 10 days			10pm	X	X	X	X	X	X	X	X	X	X	X	X	X	X	X	X	X	X	X	X	X	X	X	X	X	X	X	X	X	X	X

Special Instructions: *Reason: bronchitis*

How many Amoxicillin tablets should be split-packaged by the pharmacy and transferred to the day program staff by the residential program staff? _____

When medication administration is scheduled during school hours, residential program staff must maintain all Chain of Custody documentation. Documentation includes the use of a transfer form and the acceptable code, 'S' in the appropriate boxes on the medication administration sheet grid.

Massachusetts | Responsibilities in Action

Off-Site Medication Administration (OSA)

Off-site medication administration is defined as medication administered by you or a licensed staff, at an off-site location during the hours a person would typically receive medication in the:

- home or
- day program

Examples include, but are not limited to:

- A person who leaves their home for a community outing, the movie theater or the mall and will have their medication administered by you while attending the activity.
- A person who leaves the day program to go to their work location or to attend an activity and will have their medication administered by you during work or while attending the activity.

Preparation of Off-Site Medication

If you will be administering medication during a time period of more than 24 hours, the medication must be prepared by the pharmacy.

If the pharmacy cannot prepare the medication and you will be administering medication during a time period of less than 24 hours, you may prepare the medication.

When you prepare the off-site medication, you must also be responsible for administering the medication. Each medication strength must be

- in a separate container*
    - marked directly on the container with the information from the original pharmacy label including the
        - person's name
        - medication name
        - strength of medication
        - amount to administer
        - frequency (including specific time(s) to administer)
        - name of ordering HCP
        - directions for medication administration
        - date prepared
        - amount of medication in the OSA container (number of tablets, capsules or mL)

*A coin envelope may be used for each medication you prepare.

After Preparation of Off-Site Medication

After you prepare the OSA medication, you must document. You will write a medication progress or narrative note that includes the location of where you will administer the OSA medication and leave the corresponding medication box open.

See the documentation example below after preparation of an OSA medication.

Month and Year: March, yr — **MEDICATION ADMINISTRATION SHEET** — **Allergies: none**

Start	Generic Clonazepam		Hour	1	2	3	4	5	6	7	8	9	10	11	12	13	14	15	16	17	18	19	20	21	22	23	24	25	26	27	28	29	30	31
3/1/yr	Brand Klonopin		8am	SD	SD	SD	SD	SD																										
	Strength 1mg	Dose 1mg																																
Stop	Amount 1 tab	Route mouth	4pm	JS	AS	AS	AS																											
cont.	Frequency twice daily at 8am-4pm																																

Special instructions: *Reason: seizures*

Name   Tanisha Johnson   **MEDICATION PROGRESS NOTE**

Date	Time	Medication	Dose	Given	Not Given	Refused	Other	Reason (for giving/not giving)	Results and/or Response	Staff Signature
3/5/yr 2:10pm I prepared Tanisha's 4pm dose of Clonazepam 1mg for an OSA. I will administer the medication to her while she is attending an outing to watch a movie followed by dinner.										*Amanda Smith*

> If medication prepared for the off-site medication administration is a countable controlled medication, when subtracting, it must be noted as OSA in the Count Book.

Massachusetts | Responsibilities in Action

Documentation example after preparation of an OSA countable controlled medication in the Count Book:

3| P a g e

Name: Tanisha Johnson   _X_ Original Entry or
Doctor: Dr. Chen Lee   ___ Transferred from page___
Pharmacy: Greenleaf   Prescription Number: N236
Medication and Strength: Clonazepam 1mg   Prescription Date: March 3, yr
Directions: Take 1 tablet by mouth twice daily at 8am and 4pm

Date	Time	Route	Amount on Hand	Amount Used	Amount Left	Signature
3/3/yr	9am	Received from pharmacy			60	Sam Dowd/ Linda White
3/3/yr	4pm	Mouth	60	One	59	Jenna Sherman
3/4/yr	8am	Mouth	59	One	58	Sam Dowd
3/4/yr	4pm	Mouth	58	One	57	Amanda Smith
3/5/yr	8am	Mouth	57	One	56	Sam Dowd
3/5/yr	2pm	OSA	56	One	55	Amanda Smith

During Off-Site Medication Administration

During the off-site administration time, you must have a copy of your current MAP Certificate.

2020 The Massachusetts Departments of Public Health, Developmental Services, Mental Health, Children and Families and the Rehabilitation Commission

Return from Off-Site Medication Administration

When you return with the person to their home or day program, you must write a second medication progress or narrative note indicating the medication was administered.

Documentation example of the second medication progress note after returning to the person's home following an off-site medication administration:

Name Tanisha Johnson **MEDICATION PROGRESS NOTE** **March, yr**

Date	Time	Medication	Dose	Given	Not Given	Refused	Other	Reason (for giving/not giving)	Results and/or Response	Staff Signature
3/5/yr	2:10pm	I prepared Tanisha's 4pm dose of Clonazepam 1 mg for an OSA. I will administer the medication to her while she is attending an outing to watch a movie followed by dinner.								
										Amanda Smith
3/5/yr	7:27pm	I administered Tanisha's Clonazepam 1 mg at 4:10pm								
										Amanda Smith

The staff responsible for medication administration in the residential program when the person is away will document by writing 'OSA' in the medication box at the scheduled administration time.

Month and Year: March, yr **MEDICATION ADMINISTRATION SHEET** **Allergies: none**

Start	Generic Clonazepam			Hour	1	2	3	4	5	6	7	8	9	10	11	12	13	14	15	16	17	18	19	20	21	22	23	24	25	26	27	28	29	30	31
3/1/yr	Brand Klonopin			8am	SD	SD	SD	SD	SD																										
	Strength 1mg	Dose 1mg																																
Stop	Amount 1 tab	Route mouth		4pm	JS	AS	AS	AS	OSA																										
cont.	Frequency twice daily at 8am-4pm																																	

Special instructions: *Reason: seizures*

If for any reason the medication was not administered as ordered off-site, you must complete all necessary follow up and write a medication progress or narrative note.

Unused Off-Site Oral Medication

Any unused OSA oral medication prepared by you may not be returned for use; it must be disposed and documented in the disposal log.

Any unused OSA oral medication prepared by the pharmacy in tamper-resistant packaging may be returned for use. If it is a countable medication it must be added back into the count.

See the MAP Policy Manual for details of staffed vacation requirements.

Leave of Absence

Leave of absence (LOA) is when medication is released from a person's home to a family member or a responsible friend to administer who is not required to be MAP Certified or a licensed staff.

Preparation of LOA Medication

For any leave of absence contact the pharmacy to package the LOA medication.

The pharmacy must prepare the medication for any leave of absence if the LOA is

- scheduled ahead of time or
- greater than 72 hours

If the pharmacy is contacted and is unable to prepare the medication you may prepare it only if the LOA is

- unplanned (not scheduled ahead of time) and is
- less than 72 hours

Knowing the date and time the person will be leaving on the LOA and the date and time the person will be returning from the LOA will help to determine the amount of medication to prepare.

If staff prepares the LOA medication, each medication strength must be

- prepared in a separate container
  - marked directly on the container with the information from the original pharmacy label including the
    - person's name
    - medication name
    - strength of medication
    - amount to administer
    - frequency (including specific time(s) to administer)
    - name of ordering HCP
    - directions for medication administration (specific dosing and time)
    - date prepared
    - amount of medication in the LOA container (number of tablets, capsules or mL)

All medication sent on the LOA must be documented on a Leave of Absence form.

The Leave of Absence form must include the:

- person's name
- destination
- date and time of departure
- estimated date and time of return
- allergies
- medication name
    - strength of tablet, capsule or mL
    - frequency
    - amount to administer
    - route
    - directions or special instructions, if any
- amount of medication placed into the container
- who prepared the medication
    - pharmacy name or
    - staff name
- signature(s) of the
    - second staff, if available, who double checked the prepared LOA medication
    - staff releasing the medication and
    - family member or responsible friend accepting the medication

Written instructions and medication information should also be available to the person who is responsible for medication administration during the LOA.

Sample Leave of Absence Form

Name _____ Allergies _____ Date _____

Program address _____ Program Phone _____

Destination address _____

Date and time of departure _____

Date and time of expected return _____

Medication	Strength	Amount	Frequency	Route	Special Instructions	# Pills Provided

Medications Packaged By: Check one

☐ Pharmacy   Name of Pharmacy   _____ Date ____

☐ Staff   Name of Staff   _____ Date ____

Name of Staff who double-checked** preparation of medication: ** (if available)
_____ Date ____

I understand the above information regarding medication and its administration. My questions have been answered. I understand I may call the staff if any further questions.

Name of Person entrusted with medication   _____
Signature _____ Date ____

Name of Staff releasing medication _____
Signature _____ Date ____

The original, signed LOA form is part of a person's health record.

If the LOA medication is a countable controlled medication it must be subtracted in the Count Book as a LOA medication.

*On 2-24-yr at 10am, Amanda Smith subtracted nine tablets from the count sheet, that were prepared by the pharmacy, for a leave of absence (LOA) when those medications were released to David's sister.

1| P a g e

Name: David Cook

Doctor: Dr. Black

Pharmacy: Greenleaf

Medication and Strength: Phenobarbital 32.4mg

Directions: Take 3 tablets by mouth once daily in evening

__X__ Original Entry or

_____Transferred from page___

Prescription Number: N671

Prescription Date: Feb. 17, yr

Date	Time	Route	Amount on Hand	Amount Used	Amount Left	Signature
2/17/yr	9am	Received from Pharmacy			42	Linda White/Sam Dowd
2/17/yr	8pm	Mouth	42	Three	39	Jenna Sherman
2/18/yr	8pm	Mouth	39	Three	36	Jenna Sherman
2/19/yr	8pm	Mouth	36	Three	33	Amanda Smith
2/20/yr	8pm	Mouth	33	Three	30	Amanda Smith
2/21/yr	8pm	Mouth	30	Three	27	Amanda Smith
2/22/yr	8pm	Mouth	27	Three	24	Jenna Sherman
2/23/yr	8pm	Mouth	24	Three	21	Jenna Sherman
2/24/yr	10am	LOA	21	nine*	12	Amanda Smith
2/27/yr	8pm	Mouth	12	Three	9	Amanda Smith

Massachusetts | Responsibilities in Action

Documentation of the LOA

When the person is away on a leave of absence document by writing 'LOA' in the medication box at the scheduled administration time.

After the LOA

When the person returns to their home, staff must ask the family or the responsible friend whether all medications were administered during the LOA.

Any unused LOA oral medication may not be returned for use. The person's family or responsible friend may keep the medication for future LOA's. If not kept by the person's family or responsible friend, the LOA oral medication must be disposed and documented.

Items such as inhalers and topical ointments, etc. may be returned for use.

Ask your supervisor to review the procedure regarding staff responsibilities when a person returns home from a LOA specific to your work location.

Disposal

All controlled and countable controlled medication to be disposed must be documented on the DPH Controlled Substance Disposal Record Form.

Disposals of OTC medication and dietary supplements may also be documented using the DPH Controlled Substance Disposal Record Form.

The disposal record is a consecutive, chronological documentation of medications disposed. This means, each time a medication is disposed, it is assigned an 'item' number and dated. For example, the first disposal to take place in a new program would be documented as item #1 (year), followed by item #2 (year), item #3 (year) etc. Typically, a program will start each new calendar year with item #1 and the current year.

When documenting a medication disposal on the disposal record do not leave blank spaces. Complete the

- heading of the form including the
  - o agency name
  - o program address
  - o DPH MAP Registration number
- item #
- date of disposal
- person's name
- date the prescription was last filled
- medication name
- strength of medication
- amount disposed
- reason for disposal*
- Count Book information
  - o If the medication was a countable medication include the
    - Count Book number and
    - Count Book page number
  - o If the medication was not a countable medication
    - write 'n/a' (not applicable) in the space
- Rx number
- pharmacy name
- signature of MAP Certified supervisor
- your signature

Massachusetts | Responsibilities in Action

*When countable medications are disposed, the Disposal Record and Count Book documentation must agree including; the reason why disposal was needed; documented in both places.

Possible reasons for medication disposal include

- the medication
  - was refused
  - dropped on the floor
  - was discontinued
  - expired (outdated)
  - medication was prepared incorrectly
- the person died
- the supply of medicine in the program is more than allowed
- unused LOA oral medication was returned to the program

Medication disposals must be completed with two Certified staff, 'shoulder to shoulder', one of which is a MAP Certified Supervisor except as noted below.

Two Certified staff (no supervisor) may dispose of the medication if the medication was

- refused
- dropped
- prepared incorrectly
  - if your supervisor is unavailable and
    - if your agency allows it

Ask your Supervisor if they are required for all medication disposals or if two Certified staff (no supervisor) may dispose of a refused or dropped dose of medication, at your work location.

DPH requires that the medication to be disposed is rendered unusable, meaning once you have prepared the medication for disposal; no one is able to still use it. Look for any specific disposal instructions on the medication information sheet; if there are any, follow them.

Massachusetts | Responsibilities in Action

While there are many methods for rendering a medication unusable, typically, you will

- remove the medication from the pharmacy packaging
- put the medication into a sealable bag
- crush the medication in the sealable bag
- add dish detergent to the crushed medication
  - you can also use
    - moistened kitty litter
    - hand sanitizer
    - used coffee grounds
- seal the bag and put it into an airtight, non-descript container
- place it in the trash

Make sure all identifying personal information (pharmacy label) is removed from the empty pharmacy packaging before placing it in the trash.

Medication may not be returned to the pharmacy for disposal. There are community 'Take Back' medication disposal options.

On March 3, yr, Amanda Smith accidently dropped one tablet of Tanisha Johnson's Clonazepam 1mg on the floor and disposed of the tablet with Linda White. In this example, disposal documentation was completed in the Count Book and on the disposal form. (The pharmacy label is used to complete a disposal form.) Notice the entry fifteen minutes later when another tablet was removed for administration.

3| P a g e

Name: Tanisha Johnson   __X__ Original Entry or

Doctor: Dr. Chen Lee   _____Transferred from page__

Pharmacy: Greenleaf   Prescription Number: N236

Medication and Strength: Clonazepam 1mg   Prescription Date: March 3, yr

Directions: Take 1 tablet by mouth twice daily at 8am and 4pm

Date	Time	Route	Amount on Hand	Amount Used	Amount Left	Signature
3/3/yr	9am	Received from Pharmacy			60	John Craig/Sam Dowd
3/3/yr 4:00pm during preparation a tablet was dropped on the floor. The one tablet was disposed leaving 59 tablets. See Item#2 on disposal record.						Amanda Smith/Linda White
3/3/yr	4:15pm	mouth	59	One	58	Amanda Smith

Rx # N236	Greenleaf Pharmacy	111-222-3434	
	20 Main Street		
	Treetop, MA 00000	3/3/yr	
Tanisha Johnson			
Clonazepam 1mg		Qty. 60	
IC Klonopin			
Take 1 tablet by mouth twice daily at 8am and 4pm			
		Dr. Lee	
Lot # 365-792	ED: 3/3/yr	Refills: 3	

Massachusetts | Responsibilities in Action

Controlled Substance Disposal Record Form

Agency: Amercare   **ProgramSite:** 45 Shade St.   **DPH Registration #:** MAP 00001

Item #: 1-yr		Date: 02/18/yr	Item #:		Date:
Individual's Name: David Cook		Date Last Filled: 05/5/yr	Individual's Name:		Date Last Filled:
Medication: Tramadol		Strength: 50mg	Medication:		Strength:
Amount Disposed: twenty tabs	Take ☐ Back	Reason: DC'd	Amount Disposed:	Take ☐ Back	Reason:
Countable Controlled Substance Book Number: 1	Page Number: 7	Rx Number: N125 — Pharmacy: Greenleaf	Countable Controlled Substance Book Number:	Page Number:	Rx Number: — Pharmacy:
Signatures: Staff: Sam Dowd		Supervisor: Linda White	Signatures: Staff:		Supervisor:

Item #: 2-yr		Date: 03/3/yr	Item #:		Date:
Individual's Name: Tanisha Johnson		Date Last Filled: 03/3/yr	Individual's Name:		Date Last Filled:
Medication: Clonazepam		Strength: 1mg	Medication:		Strength:
Amount Disposed: one tab	Take ☐ Back	Reason: fell on floor	Amount Disposed:	Take ☐ Back	Reason:
Countable Controlled Substance Book Number: 1	Page Number: 3	Rx Number: N236 — Pharmacy: Greenleaf	Countable Controlled Substance Book Number:	Page Number:	Rx Number: — Pharmacy:
Signatures: Staff: Amanda Smith		Supervisor: Linda White	Signatures: Staff:		Supervisor:

Item #:		Date:	Item #:		Date:
Individual's Name:		Date Last Filled:	Individual's Name:		Date Last Filled:
Medication:		Strength:	Medication:		Strength:
Amount Disposed:	Take ☐ Back	Reason:	Amount Disposed:	Take ☐ Back	Reason:
Countable Controlled Substance Book Number:	Page Number:	Rx Number: — Pharmacy:	Countable Controlled Substance Book Number:	Page Number:	Rx Number: — Pharmacy:
Signatures: Staff:		Supervisor:	Signatures: Staff:		Supervisor:

Destruction of all prescription medications in Schedules II -VI that are either outdated, spoiled or have not been administered due to a change in the prescription or a stop order shall be documented on the DPH approved disposal record. According to regulations at 105CMR 700.003(f)(3)(c): "Disposal occurs in the presence of at least two witnesses and in accordance with any policies at the Department of Public Health". DPH policy requires disposal to occur in the presence of two Certified or licensed staff of which one of the two is supervisory staff. If a supervisor is unavailable when an individual refuses a prepared medication, or a pill is inadvertently dropped then two Certified staff may render these medications unusable in accordance with acceptable DPH disposal practices. Failure to maintain complete and accurate records of drug destruction could result in revocation of your Controlled Substance Registration. Disposal must render the medication unusable and must be in accordance with acceptable DPH disposal practices. Unless prohibited by local ordinance, acceptable practices include, but are not limited to, flushing (flushing should be restricted to those medications so labeled), crushing the medication and/or dissolving in water put into a sealable bag and mixing with an unpalatable substance (such as liquid soap, used coffee grounds, kitty litter). Mixture should then be put into an impermeable, non-descript container, (e.g., detergent bottle) and placed in trash. Medications are not permitted to be returned to the pharmacy for destruction. Medications returned to the program site (e.g., LOAs) must be destroyed as per DPH regulation. They cannot be reused by the program.

Page # 1

2020 The Massachusetts Departments of Public Health, Developmental Services, Mental Health, Children and Families and the Rehabilitation Commission

If the medication to be disposed is a countable medication, the countable medication must remain on count until the disposal is completed.

This means, if you subtracted the medication in the Count Book and then the person refused the medication, if a second certified or licensed staff is not available; keep the medication on count until a second staff is available to complete the disposal process. After the medication is disposed you may subtract the medication from the count.

Fill in the blanks

1. Medication disposal must take place with _____ Certified staff.

2. When a countable medication is disposed, it must be documented on a disposal record and in the _____ _____

3. On a disposal record, the _____ _____ is the chronological numbering of medications disposed.

4. A MAP Certified _____ must be present when disposing of expired or discontinued medications.

Blister Pack Monitoring

Although not a MAP requirement, if used at your program you will

- document medication was removed from a blister pack by writing your
    - initials, the date and the time on the back of the blister pack
        - for each tablet removed.

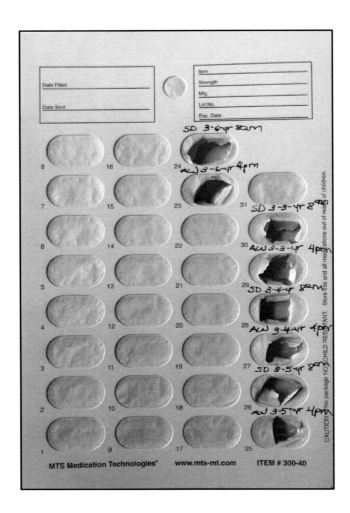

When blister pack monitoring is used at your work location, you should look at the set of documentation before yours. If you notice there is no documentation for an earlier dose of medication that should have been administered by a previous staff, contact a MAP Consultant immediately.

In addition, your supervisor or a designee will periodically review the documentation on the back of the blister pack to ensure medication was given as prescribed.

Medication Supply Discrepancy

Suspicious

A suspicious count discrepancy is when the count is off and there is suspicion of loss, diversion (theft), tampering or inconsistencies with documentation. These discrepancies are known as a loss of medication or a drug loss. They are serious and can result in potential criminal prosecution.

- Loss is when a medication is unaccounted for at either a program or a pharmacy
- Diversion (theft) is taking from a persons' medication for a use other than the person
- Tampering is altering or substituting a medication or the packaging of a medication
- Documentation inconsistencies specific to this subject include, but are not limited to:
  - o medication documented as disposed and later discovered as not disposed
  - o altered legal documents (HCP orders, medication sheets, etc.)
  - o a disposal record that contains only one staff signature

Prescription medication losses (schedules II-VI) must be reported to the Drug Control Program (DCP) within 24 hours after discovery of the medication loss using the DPH/DCP Drug Incident Report (DIR) Form.

If tampering is suspected:

- Call the persons HCP and the local police
- Complete a DIR
- Follow any instructions given to you by the HCP, the police or the DCP

In addition, the suspected tampered medication must be removed from the medication storage area. If the medication is a countable medication it should be removed from the count and documented as such including the reason why. The medication should be secured in an area or container on site that only your supervisor has access to.

- o Do not remove the medication from the home,
  - ▪ doing so breaks the chain of custody.

If the medication is transferred to the police or to a DCP investigator, complete a transfer form.

If the medication is not transferred from the home to an enforcement representative, the medication may be disposed following MAP policy once the investigation is complete.

If loss, theft, or documentation inconsistencies are suspected, your supervisor must be contacted. A DIR form must be completed.

Remember, documentation tells a story from beginning to end. If a suspicious discrepancy is noted in the Count Book, it must be documented accurately, using as many lines as needed, to 'tell the story' of what happened. Make sure your documentation includes that the discrepancy was reported to the DPH/DCP and your supervisor.

11| P a g e

Name: Ellen Tracey

Doctor: Dr. Glass

Pharmacy: Greenleaf

Medication and Strength: Lorazepam 0.5mg

Directions: Take 2 tablets by mouth twice daily and 1 tablet by mouth once daily PRN, anxiety. Give PRN dose at least 4 hours apart from scheduled dose. See Support Plan.

____ Original Entry or

_X__ Transferred from page_5_

Prescription Number: N448

Prescription Date: April 1, yr

Date	Time	Route	Amount on Hand	Amount Used	Amount Left	Signature
4/15/yr	9am	Received from Pharmacy			18	Linda White / Sam Dowd
4/15/yr	8pm	Mouth	18	Two	16	Amanda Smith
4/16/yr	8am	Mouth	16	Two	14	Sam Dowd
4/16/yr	3pm	Mouth	14	One	13	Sam Dowd
4/16/yr 3:51pm there are 12 tabs in the package. Blister pack monitoring review shows documentation is completed for the last dose administered. There is one empty bubble after the 4/16/yr 3pm dose for anxiety. There are no initials, date or time documented near the empty bubble. Linda White, Supervisor notified. Amanda Smith					
4/16/yr	8pm	Mouth	12	Two	10	Amanda Smith
4/16/yr 9pm Drug Incident Report form faxed to DPH. Linda White					

Massachusetts | Responsibilities in Action

208

Count Signature Sheet

Date	Time	Count correct yes/no	Incoming Staff	Outgoing Staff
4/15/yr	7:19am	yes	Amanda Smith	Sam Dowd
4/15/yr	3:10pm	yes	Jenna Sherman	Amanda Smith
4/15/yr	11:06pm	yes	single person count	Jenna Sherman
4/16/yr	10:12am	yes	Sam Dowd	Linda White (witness)
4/16/yr	3:57pm	No	Amanda Smith	Sam Dowd
During the count, one of Ellen Tracey's Lorazepam 0.5 mg tab seems to be missing. See count sheet page 11. There are 12 tabs in the package. Blister pack monitoring review shows documentation is completed for the last dose administered. There is one empty bubble after the 4/16/yr 3pm dose for anxiety. There are no initials, date or time documented near the empty bubble. Linda White, Supervisor notified. Drug Incident report form to be completed and faxed to DPH. ——————————————— Amanda Smith				
4/16/yr 9pm Drug Incident Report form faxed to DPH. Linda White				
4/16/yr	11:07pm	yes	Jenna Sherman	Amanda Smith

In the event of a countable medication loss, the count signature sheet will reflect that the count is incorrect; you will document 'no'. When noting that the count is incorrect, you must also include the corresponding count sheet page number where the loss was discovered.

Department of Public Health
Drug Control Program
Drug Incident Report

Please note that any box framed in red is a 'mandatory' field - it must be filled in before submitting the report.

Pursuant to the Department's regulations at 105 CMR 700.005(D), registrants are required to report the loss of any controlled substances upon discovery. When a drug loss is discovered, kindly fill out this incident report and email it to the Drug Control Program at DIR.DCP@state.ma.us within twenty four hours of discovery. Do not include any Personally Identifiable Information (PII) in this report.

Date of Report	Report Prepared By	
Title	Contact's Phone (10 digit number) ext	Contact's e-mail

Facility Information

Facility Name

Address

City	County	Zip Code	+ 4

Facility Type

Date of Loss	Specific location of loss (unit, floor, etc., if applicable)

Incident Type

☐ Diversion   ☐ Loss   ☐ Theft   ☐ Tampering   ☐ Documentation

☐ Other (Please Specify) _____

List drugs (use additional entries on the back of this form if necessary)

To select a drug begin typing in the name of the drug (brand or generic). As the options narrow, select the correct drug from the drop down list at any time. If the drug you are looking for does not appear, you may enter 'other' - whereupon a text box will open up for you to enter the name of the drug.

Once you have entered/selected a drug, hit the 'tab' key to move to the 'Qty' box. Please note that the Qty, Strength and Dosage Form boxes will be 'locked out' until a drug has been selected.

Drug	Qty	Strength	Dosage Form

Narrative (Please explain what happened, what factors may have contributed to loss, and any other relevant information. Please indicate if patient harm was involved. Please use additional sheets if necessary.)

Drug Incident Report   **Submit**   R20190915-01

Non-suspicious

A non-suspicious count discrepancy is when the count is off however it can be easily resolved by checking the addition and/or subtraction documented. If a non-suspicious discrepancy is noted in the Count Book it must be corrected accurately, using as many lines as needed to 'tell the story' of what happened. Make sure your documentation also includes that you reported the discrepancy and correction to your supervisor.

1|Page

Name: David Cook   __X__ Original Entry or

Doctor: Dr. Black   _____Transferred from page___

Pharmacy: Greenleaf   Prescription Number: N671

Medication and Strength: Phenobarbital 32.4mg   Prescription Date: Feb. 15, yr

Directions: Take 3 tablets by mouth once daily in evening

Date	Time	Route	Amount on Hand	Amount Used	Amount Left	Signature
2/15/yr	9am	Received from Pharmacy			42	Linda White/Sam Dowd
2/15/yr	8pm	Mouth	42	Three	39	Jenna Sherman
2/16/yr	8pm	Mouth	39	Three	36	Jenna Sherman
2/17/yr	8pm	Mouth	36	Three	33	Amanda Smith
2/18/yr	8pm	Mouth	33	Three	30	Amanda Smith
2/19/yr	8pm	Mouth	30	Three	27	Amanda Smith
2/20/yr	8pm	Mouth	27	Three	24	Jenna Sherman
2/21/yr	8pm	Mouth	24	Three	21	Jenna Sherman
2/22/yr	10am	LOA	21	nine*	12	Amanda Smith
2/25/yr	8pm	Mouth	12	Three	9	Amanda Smith
2/26/yr	8pm	Mouth	9	Three	5	Jenna Sherman
2-27-yr 10am When counting I noticed the amount left says 5 but the number in the medication package is 6. The math of the 2-26-yr at 8pm entry is incorrect. I notified Linda White, Supervisor. Correct count is 6						
					6	Sam Dowd

Massachusetts | Responsibilities in Action   212

Your role in the Chain of Custody is necessary to ensure the security of the medication. Just like the links of a chain, each joined to the other; the 'Chain of Custody' documentation trail of medication received into or transferred out of your program must never be broken.

Let's Review

- All medications and dietary supplements must be accounted for and tracked
- Medications are tracked using:
    - Pharmacy Ordering and Receiving Log
    - Pharmacy receipts
    - Medication sheets
    - Count Book
    - Transfer form
    - LOA form
    - Disposal Record
    - Blister Pack Monitoring (if used at your agency)
- Always
    - complete the appropriate tracking document
    - include your signature and date
- If releasing medication to another person, make sure to obtain their signature as accepting the medication
- Countable medication must be reconciled (counted) every time the medication storage keys change hands
- Diversion (theft) of prescription medication may result in potential criminal prosecution
- Prescription medication losses must be reported to DPH/DCP within 24 hours after discovery of the loss
- You play an important role in maintaining the Chain of Custody

Unit 9

Medication Occurrences

Responsibilities you will learn

- The definition of a medication occurrence
- What you do if you make or discover a medication occurrence
- When and how to report a medication occurrence
- How to help reduce medication occurrences

As you have learned, to administer medication safely, the process must be completed from beginning to end while being mindful. Most medication occurrences can be traced to not following the steps of the medication administration process.

A **medication occurrence** is when one of the 5 rights goes wrong during medication administration, including:

- Wrong
    - person
    - medication
    - dose
    - time
        - omission (a subcategory of wrong time)
    - route

A Medication Occurrence Report (MOR) is a document used to track and report each time one of the 5 rights goes wrong during medication administration.

A **hotline medication occurrence** is when medical intervention (including but not limited to lab work, tests, Emergency Room visit, HCP visit, etc.), illness, injury or death follow the medication occurrence.

Ask your Supervisor how MORs are submitted at your work location.

Procedure Following a Medication Occurrence

As soon as a medication occurrence is identified (whether you make it or discover it) you must:

- Check to see if the person is ok

- If not ok, call 911
    - You must know your agency's emergency procedures and where emergency contact information is located

- Call a MAP Consultant
    - When speaking to the MAP Consultant, make sure you
        - tell the MAP Consultant exactly what happened, including
            - the medication(s) involved
            - the total number of doses involved
            - what type of occurrence happened
            - date and time of occurrence

- Follow all recommendations given to you by the MAP Consultant

- Notify your supervisor

- Document in medication administration record
    - what happened
    - who you notified
        - include the MAP Consultant's full name
        - your supervisor's full name
    - the MAP Consultant's recommendations
    - what you did (the MAP Consultant's recommendations)
    - sign your name
    - date/time

- Complete a Medication Occurrence Report (MOR)
    - if the medication occurrence is a Hotline Medication Occurrence
        - notify DPH and the MAP Coordinator within 24 hours of discovery of the medication occurrence
            - fax and telephone numbers for DPH are located on the MOR form
    - submit the report within 7 days of discovery of the medication occurrence
        - to the MAP Coordinator

Massachusetts | Responsibilities in Action   215

2020 The Massachusetts Departments of Public Health, Developmental Services, Mental Health, Children and Families and the Rehabilitation Commission

Department of Public Health Medication Administration Program
MEDICATION OCCURRENCE REPORT (side one)

Agency Name		Date of Discovery	
Individual's Name		Time of Discovery	
Site Address (street)		Date(s) of Occurrence	
City/Town Zip Code		Time(s) of Occurrence	
Site Telephone No.		DPH Registration No.	MAP

A)   Type Of Occurrence (As per regulation, contact MAP Consultant)

1 ☐ Wrong Individual   4 ☐ Wrong Medication (includes medication given without an order)
2 ☐ Wrong Dose   5 ☐ Wrong Time (includes medication not given in appropriate timeframe)
3 ☐ Wrong Route   ☐ Omission (subgroup of 'wrong time'--medication not given or forgotten)

B)   Medication(s) Involved

	Medication Name	Dosage	Frequency/Time	Route
As Ordered:				
As Given:				
As Ordered:				
As Given:				
As Ordered:				
As Given:				

C)   MAP Consultant Contacted (Check all that apply)

Type	Name	Date Contacted	Time Contacted
☐ Registered Nurse			
☐ Registered Pharmacist			
☐ Health Care Provider			

D)   Hotline Events

of the events below follow the occurrence? ☐ Yes ☐ No

If yes, check all that apply below, and within 24 hours of discovery fax this form to DPH (617) 753-8046 or call to notify DPH at (617) 983-6782 and notify your DMH/DCF or DDS MAP Coordinator.
For All Occurrences, forward reports to your DMH/DCF or DDS MAP Coordinator within 7 days.

☐ Medical Intervention (see Section E below)   ☐ Illness   ☐ Injury   ☐ Death

E)   MAP Consultant's Recommended Action

Medical Intervention   ☐ Yes ☐ No   If Yes, Check all that apply.

☐ Health Care Provider Visit	☐ Lab Work or Other Tests	☐ Clinic Visit
☐ Emergency Room Visit	☐ Hospitalization	

☐ Other: Please describe

F)   Supervisory Review/Follow-up
Contributing Factors: Check all that apply.

1 ☐ Failure to Properly Document Administration

2 ☐ Medication not Available (Explain Below)

3a ☐ Medication Administered by Non-Certified Staff (includes instances of expired or revoked Certification)

3b ☐ Medication Administered by a licensed nurse, employed on site. LPN ☐ RN ☐

3c ☐ Medication Administered by a licensed nurse, not employed on site (e.g., VNA)

4 ☐ Improperly Labeled by Pharmacy

5 ☐ Failure to Accurately Record and/or Transcribe an Order

6 ☐ Failure to Accurately Take or Receive a Telephone Order

7 ☐ Medication Had Been Discontinued

8 ☐ Other (Narrative Required)

Narrative: (If additional space is required, continue in box F-1)

Print Name	**Print Title**	**Date**
Contact phone number	**E-mail address**	

2020 The Massachusetts Departments of Public Health, Developmental Services, Mental Health, Children and Families and the Rehabilitation Commission

Massachusetts | Responsibilities in Action   216

The DPH Medication Occurrence Report form is used for all MORs in DMH-DCF programs and in DDS programs for hotlines only.

Medication occurrences provide an opportunity to improve medication administration procedures. When reviewing medication occurrences, it is important to focus on what contributed to the occurrence rather than who made the occurrence.

Every staff can and should learn from someone else's mistake. If you make a mistake when administering medication, it is extremely important to remember that the safety of the person must always be your primary concern and to report the occurrence to the MAP Consultant immediately.

The chances of a medication occurrence happening can be greatly decreased by always following the medication administration process you learned in this curriculum. Follow the same process each time you administer medication.

Ask your supervisor what the policy/procedure is regarding medication occurrence follow up specific to your work location. Expect that if you discover or make an occurrence your supervisor will speak to you to learn about the circumstances of what happened. A supervisor does this to determine if the:

- occurrence was reported promptly to the MAP consultant
- MAP consultant responded in a timely manner
- recommendation was followed

In addition a supervisor reviews:

- if there was an impact on the person
- the completed medication occurrence report
    - which of the five rights of medication administration were violated
        - right person
        - right medication
        - right dose
        - right time
            - omission

- right route
- the form was forwarded to the office, if necessary

It is important for a supervisor to know:

- Was the HCP order current?
- Was the HCP order clearly understood?
- Was the HCP order posted and verified before the medication was given?
- Was the proper procedure used to assure the identity of the person?
- Were three checks for the five rights conducted before the medication was administered?
- Was the medication transcribed correctly?
- Was the medication sheet filled out correctly?
- Was the pharmacy label legible and clearly understood?
- Was the correct medication available to be given?
- Was the prepared medication kept secure (under Certified staff's control) until the intended person swallowed the medication?

Gathering this information will help a supervisor determine the reason for an occurrence. Reasons for an occurrence may be:

- Failure to follow the medication administration process
- Failure to follow the correct process in ordering and receiving medication
- Contributing environmental factors such as a:
  o snow storm
- Documentation errors such as a:
  o transcription error
- Other contributing factors such as:
  o noise

Gathering this information helps a supervisor determine any corrective action such as:

- Reviewing procedures with the staff (retraining specific to what went wrong)
- Reviewing regulations and/or policy with the staff (retraining specific to what went wrong)
- Requiring complete formal retraining such as:
  o Repeating a full MAP Certification training
- Providing 1:1 supervision practice until the supervisor is satisfied of correct practice such as:
  o supervised medication passes
- Disciplinary action

Other responses may be necessary when the staff member participation in a medication occurrence was only a partial cause of the occurrence (certain types of pharmacy error, HCP error, etc.)

Number the 'Procedure Following a Medication Occurrence' in the order to be completed if you make or discover a medication occurrence.

A. __ Complete a Medication Occurrence Report

B. __ Follow all recommendations given to you by the MAP Consultant

C. __ Notify your supervisor

D. __ Call 911, if needed

E. __ Document what you did and who you notified

F. __ Call a MAP Consultant

G. __ Check to see if the person is ok

Massachusetts | Responsibilities in Action

A **wrong person** medication occurrence means the medication was administered

- to the wrong person, either by
    - o misidentification
    - o distraction
    - o the medication was left unattended or not secured and someone else ingested it

To minimize the chances of a medication occurrence involving a wrong person, always

- remain mindful
    - o Think about what you are doing as you prepare medication; do not rush or skip steps to save time
    - o If possible, bring the person to the medication area
    - o If you are unsure of who the person is, ask another staff who is familiar with the person or look at the Emergency Fact Sheet picture
    - o Do not try to do more than one task at the same time
        - For example
            - Do not prepare medication while talking on your cell phone
    - o Never leave medication unattended
        - if the medication is refused, secure it until you attempt a second or third administration
    - o Never pre-pour medication

You and your coworker Jim will be working together; Jim is assigned medication administration duties and you are assigned morning hygiene. To save time, Jim decides to 'pre-pour' all of the medications.

Just as Jim finishes preparing all of the medications, he hears you call for 'Help!' Jim goes to help you leaving the prepared medication unattended. When Jim returns to the medication area he finds one of the people living in the home with the empty pill cups.

1. What category of medication occurrence was made? _____
2. What should Jim do next? _____
3. How could this medication occurrence have been prevented? _____
4. What if the same scenario occurred, except Jim had correctly prepared only one set of medication; what could he have done when he heard the call for help?

_____

Massachusetts | Responsibilities in Action   220

A **wrong medication** occurrence means the medication was administered

- without a HCP order
  - including administering a medication
    - using an expired HCP order
    - that had been discontinued
    - past the stop date of a time limited medication order
    - administering one medication instead of another
      - Tegretol is ordered/Tylenol is administered instead

To minimize the chances of a medication occurrence involving a wrong medication, always

- look at the HCP order (check #1 of the medication administration process)
  - to ensure
    - it is valid; signed and dated by the HCP
    - the medication order has not been changed or was discontinued
    - what is printed on the pharmacy label is what the HCP ordered
- call a MAP Consultant if you have a question regarding a HCP order

Janet is assigned medication administration duties. She remembers from the last time she worked that Tanisha has an HCP order for Kenalog 0.1% cream to be applied to the bottoms of both feet at bedtime.

As Janet helps Tanisha get ready for bed, she gets the cream from the medication storage area and applies it to the bottom of Tanisha's feet. Janet then washes her hands and starts to prepare Tanisha's oral medications.

As Janet is reviewing Tanisha's HCP orders and medications sheets she notices that the order for the Kenalog cream was discontinued yesterday.

1. What category of medication occurrence was made? _____
2. What should Janet do next? _____
3. How could Janet have prevented this medication occurrence? _____

A **wrong dose** medication occurrence means

- too much or
- too little
  - of the medication was administered at the scheduled time

To minimize the chances of a medication occurrence involving a wrong dose, always

- look at the
  - HCP order to find the dose of the medication
  - pharmacy label to find the strength of the tablet and the amount to give to equal the dose
  - medication you have prepared in the cup to ensure the amount is correct
  - blister pack (if used) to ensure the tablet was popped out and did not 'stick' to the foil seal
  - OPUS cassette (if used) to ensure the tablet was removed and did not 'stick' in the corner
- call a MAP Consultant if the strength of tablet and amount to give does not equal the dose ordered by the HCP

Tanisha Johnson has a HCP order for Phenobarbital 64.8 mg once daily in the evening. The pharmacy had been supplying a 32.4 mg tablet with directions to take 2 tablets. When the new refill was obtained, it was supplied as a 64.8 mg tablet with directions to take 1 tablet.

At 8pm, Serena starts to prepare Tanisha's medications. Serena remembers that Tanisha always receives 2 tablets of Phenobarbital, so she gets the blister pack of Phenobarbital, pops 2 tablets and administers them.

As Serena starts to document on the medication sheet and Count Book, she notices that the strength of the tablet and amount to give has changed.

1. What category of medication occurrence was made? _____
2. What should be done next? _____
3. How could this medication occurrence have been prevented? _____

Massachusetts | Responsibilities in Action 222

A **wrong time** medication occurrence means the medication was administered

- too early (more than 1 hour before the scheduled time),
- too late (more than 1 hour after the scheduled time), or
- parameters or instructions for use of the medication were not followed

A subcategory of wrong time is

- o **Omission**
  - Meaning the medication was not administered; either it was
    - forgotten or
    - not available to administer

To minimize the chances of a medication occurrence involving a wrong time or omission, always

- use the top two boxes on the medication sheet to schedule 'am' medication times and the bottom two boxes to schedule 'pm' medication times
- administer medication within one hour before and up to one hour after, the time listed on the medication sheet
- administer PRN medication at the exact frequency ordered keeping in mind the last time it was administered
  - o there is no 1 hour window for PRN medication
- call a MAP Consultant if you have questions about the frequency of a medication
- document after administering the medication
  - o to minimize the chance of a second staff giving the medication again because there was a 'blank space' on the medication sheet and they were within the hour time window
- follow the instructions and/or parameters for use of the medication as ordered by the HCP
  - o Such as blood pressure monitoring, ordered to be taken prior to the administration of a medication
    - If the medication is administered without obtaining the blood pressure, it is a 'wrong time' medication occurrence
- ensure that medication is obtained from the pharmacy
  - o Order refills from the pharmacy at least one week before the medication runs out
  - o As soon as the last remaining refill is called into the pharmacy, notify the HCP that additional refills are needed

Massachusetts | Responsibilities in Action   223

- Be aware, the process of obtaining medication from the pharmacy may take several phone calls and is not complete until the medication is obtained

Ask your Supervisor to explain the system for obtaining refills in your work location.

You are assigned medication administration duties. You wash your hands, unlock the medication storage area, look in the medication book and see that the person has Tegretol 400mg due at 4pm; however, when you locate the blister pack of Tegretol you find the blister pack is empty.

You check the medication storage area for a backup supply and none is found. You call the pharmacy, but the pharmacist tells you there are no refills left.

1. What should you do next? _____
2. If no medication is obtained, who should you call? _____
3. What category of medication occurrence was made? _____
4. How could this medication occurrence have been prevented? _____

If after ordering a refill you have been told it was too soon to obtain the medication, contact your Supervisor. The Supervisor will review medication administrations compared to the amount received from the pharmacy to determine if too much medication was administered.

Massachusetts | Responsibilities in Action   224

A **wrong route** medication occurrence means the medication was administered

- by a way (route) not ordered by the HCP

To minimize the chances of a medication occurrence involving a wrong route, always

- look at the
    - HCP order to see the route of administration ordered
    - pharmacy label and medication sheet to ensure the route of administration is listed and is the same as the HCP order
- separate medications by their route, in the person's medication storage area
- remain mindful
    - to ensure you administer the medication by the correct route
    - call a MAP Consultant if you have questions about the way a medication is to be administered

Ellen Tracey has a HCP order for Debrox eardrops, 4 drops to each ear at bedtime and a second HCP order for Saline eye drops, 4 drops to each eye, at bedtime.

As Joe is preparing Ellen's medications, another staff is talking to Joe about the new 'app' he installed on his phone. Joe is very interested in the new 'app' and stops paying attention to what he is doing. Instead of reaching for the Saline eye drops he takes the Debrox eardrops.

Joe proceeds to administer the Debrox eardrops into Ellen's eyes. Joe realizes what he has done as he is completing a 'look back' while signing the medication sheet.

1. What category of medication occurrence was made? _____
2. What should Joe do next? _____
3. How could this medication occurrence have been prevented? _____

Match the term to the corresponding example

1.___	Wrong dose	A	Ear drops ordered for the right ear were administered into the left ear
2.___	Wrong person	B	A morning dose of medication was administered in the evening
3.___	Wrong route	C	Klonopin 2mg was ordered and Klonopin 1mg was administered
4.___	Wrong medication	D	A discontinued medication was administered
5.___	Wrong time	E	Medication ordered was not administered
6.___	Omission	F	Medication was left unattended and then was ingested by another person

Let's Review

- A medication occurrence is when one of the 5 rights goes wrong
- You must know your agency's emergency procedures and where emergency contact numbers are listed
- If you make or discover a medication occurrence speak to a MAP Consultant immediately
    - Follow all recommendations
    - Document recommendations
- The safety of the person must always be your first concern, call 911 if needed
- Medication occurrences should be viewed as 'teachable moments'
    - learn from yours and/or someone else's mistake
- Always remain mindful during the medication administration process
    - Do not try to do additional tasks, such as answering the phone or talking to a co-worker, while administering medication
- Medication occurrences must be reported to the MAP Coordinator within 7 days of discovery
- Hotline medication occurrences must be reported to DPH and the MAP Coordinator within 24 hours of discovery

Appendix

This section includes sample documentation specific to common issues that you may encounter at your work location.

Health Care Provider Order
Certified and/or licensed staff cannot alter any information recorded on a HCP order other than documenting in the margin the discontinuance of a medication, as applicable.

Pharmacy Label
Certified and/or licensed staff cannot alter the information printed on a pharmacy label. A directions change sticker may be applied next to the pharmacy label directions if criteria have been met to exhaust a current supply of medication.

Medication Sheet
On the medication sheet, all medication boxes, for scheduled times, must be initialed in real time. If documentation is completed accurately, all medication boxes will be initialed by the end of the month and there will be no blank spaces.

Late Entry Documentation
It is sometimes necessary to complete documentation after the time when it should have been completed. A late entry is an acceptable method of correcting documentation. A late entry is a progress note written well after a task was completed and tells a story of what happened earlier. A late entry includes, but is not limited to:

- date
- time
- explanation
- signature

Real Time
Real time is the actual time, to the minute (what you see on the clock). Real time documentation should occur when documenting a medication progress note, narrative note or count signature page after conducting a two person 'shoulder to shoulder' count, etc.

Massachusetts | Responsibilities in Action

Documentation Quick Guide

The Right Way	What Not To Do	Why
Use blue or black ink. Write clearly, using complete sentences.	Never use a pencil.	Medication sheets, progress notes, HCP orders, etc. are legal documents. Others need to be able to read your handwriting.
Begin each entry with the date and time; end with your signature.	Never wait to document important changes.	Documentation will reflect the correct sequence of events.
Correct errors as soon as possible.	Never try to 'squeeze in' or mark over information	Errors in documentation may lead to errors in care if not corrected promptly.
Use a 'late entry' to clarify information written earlier or to clarify a task that was not documented initially.	Never skip or leave a blank space for another staff to document later. Never post-date an entry.	Late entries will explain (tell the story) of what happened earlier.
Use only objective (factual) and subjective (how a person tells you they are feeling) observations.	Never guess or document your own hunches.	Documentation must be factual and correct to ensure a person receives the best care possible.
Draw a single line through an error. Write 'error' and your initials.	Never erase, mark over or use 'white-out'.	Documentation must be legible. Doing so can be viewed as an attempt to hide something.
Spell out information when documenting. Only use acceptable codes or abbreviations.	Never create your own documentation short cuts.	Doing so prevents others from misunderstanding what you write.
Only document and sign for a task you actually perform, such as when participating in a 'shoulder to shoulder' count or a disposal.	Never sign your signature on a count signature sheet or disposal form, etc. if you were not part of the process.	You are responsible for the information you write; doing so protects you.
Draw a line from the end of your documentation to your signature.	Never leave blank spaces.	Someone else can add incorrect information in front of your signature.
Document only for yourself.	Never document for someone else or cross out someone else's documentation.	You are responsible for the information you write.

Massachusetts | Responsibilities in Action 228

2020 The Massachusetts Departments of Public Health, Developmental Services, Mental Health, Children and Families and the Rehabilitation Commission

Requirement: All HCP orders must be posted and verified including when the HCP notes, 'no new orders' or 'no medication changes'.

Scenario: You have returned from a HCP visit with Juanita. The HCP wrote 'no medication changes' on the HCP order form.

Responsibility: You will post the HCP order, document the visit in her health record and communicate the information to others. A second staff will verify the order.

HEALTH CARE PROVIDER ORDER

Name: Juanita Gomez	**Date:** June 22, yr
Health Care Provider: Dr. David Jones	**Allergies:** Bactrim
Reason for Visit: Follow up visit after upper respiratory infection	
Current Medications: Colace liquid 200mg by mouth twice daily Dilantin 200mg by mouth twice daily Ultram 50mg by mouth twice daily	
Staff Signature: Sam Dowd	**Date:** June 22, yr
Health Care Provider Findings:	
Medication/Treatment Orders: No medication changes	
Instructions:	
Follow-up visit:	**Lab work or Tests:**
Signature: Dr. David Jones	**Date:** June 22, yr

Posted by: Sam Dowd Date: 6/22/yr Time: 1:15pm Verified by: Linda White Date: 6/22/yr Time: 2pm

Massachusetts | Responsibilities in Action

Requirement: At times, a HCP discontinues a medication or changes a medication dose or frequency. If that change is written on an order form other than the existing HCP order form listing all current medications, Certified staff should indicate the discontinuance or change on the existing HCP order form.

Scenario: You have received a fax HCP order on 12-1-yr for Juanita to D/C Colace liquid 200mg by mouth twice daily.

Responsibility: You will mark the Colace as discontinued (D/C) on the medication sheet and post and verify the fax order. Then on the existing HCP order that lists current medications, you will write in the margin next to the Colace, D/C, your initials and the date.

HEALTH CARE PROVIDER ORDER

Name: Juanita Gomez	**Date:** Sept. 29, yr
Health Care Provider: Dr. David Jones	**Allergies:** Bactrim
Reason for Visit:	
Current Medications:	
Staff Signature: Sam Dowd	**Date:** Sept. 29, yr
Health Care Provider Findings:	
Medication/Treatment Orders: Colace liquid 200mg by mouth twice daily Dilantin 200mg by mouth twice daily Ultram 50mg by mouth twice daily	
Instructions:	
Follow-up visit:	**Lab work or Tests:**
Signature: Dr. David Jones	**Date:** Sept. 29, yr

D/C'd 12/1/yr SD

Posted by: Sam Dowd Date: 9/29/yr Time: 3:15pm Verified by: Linda White Date: 9/29/yr Time: 5pm

Requirement: The medication box is initialed after medication is administered. A countable medication is subtracted from a count sheet page after removal.

Scenario: You notice a blank space on a medication sheet during your shift. The corresponding count sheet page for the same medication has no documentation that the medication was removed from the package. The staff responsible for the earlier medication administration has left work for the day.

Responsibility: You call the MAP Consultant first and then your Supervisor. You report that based on your review of the blister package, an empty bubble is marked with initials, a date and a time by the staff responsible for the earlier medication administration. The medication box and count sheet documentation are blank. It is recommended that you write a medication progress note and on the count sheet explaining what you saw, whom you contacted and what you did.

The staff who did not document after medication administration must write a 'late entry' on the medication progress note and on the corresponding count sheet the next time they are working. The medication box stays empty.

Month and Year: March, yr — **MEDICATION ADMINISTRATION SHEET** — **Allergies: none**

		Hour	1	2	3	4	5	6	7	8	9	10	11	12	13	14	15	16	17	18	19	20	21	22	23	24	25	26	27	28	29	30	31
Start 8/31/yr	Generic Clonazepam Brand Klonopin	8am	JS	JS	JS	JC	JC	JS	JS	JS	JS		JS	JS																				
	Strength 1mg Dose 1mg																																	
Stop	Amount 1 tab Route mouth	4pm	7M	SD	SD	AS	AS	SD	SD	SD	AS	SD	AS																					
Cont	Frequency twice daily 8am and 4pm																																	

Special instructions: *Reason: seizures*

Name   Tanisha Johnson   **MEDICATION PROGRESS NOTE**

Date	Time	Medication	Dose	Given	Not Given	Refused	Other	Reason (for giving/not giving)	Results and/or Response	Staff Signature
3-10-yr 3:45pm The medication box for Tanisha's 3-10-yr 8:00am dose of Clonazepam is blank. I contacted Rebecca Long, RN, MAP Consultant. Rebecca recommended checking the blister pack and count book. Documentation on the blister pack was checked. The empty bubble is initialed with the date and time on the back of the blister pack. It was not subtracted in the count book. Linda White, Supervisor was notified. ———————————————————— Sam Dowd										
3-11-yr 10:30am Late entry. Tanisha's 3-10-yr 8:00am dose of Clonazepam was given as ordered. It was not documented at that time. Jenna Sherman										

Massachusetts | Responsibilities in Action   231

2020 The Massachusetts Departments of Public Health, Developmental Services, Mental Health, Children and Families and the Rehabilitation Commission

10| P a g e

Name: Tanisha Johnson   ____ Original Entry or
Doctor: Dr. Chen Lee   _X_ Transferred from page 3
Pharmacy: Greenleaf   Prescription Number: N236
Medication and Strength: Clonazepam 1mg   Prescription Date: March 3, yr
Directions: Take 1 tablet by mouth twice daily at 8am and 4pm

Date	Time	Route	Amount on Hand	Amount Used	Amount Left	Signature
3/9/yr	9am		Page Transfer		60	John Craig/Sam Dowd
3/9/yr	4pm	Mouth	60	one	59	Amanda Smith
3/10/yr 3:51pm The morning dose was not subtracted when it was removed. I contacted Linda White, Supervisor and told her the amount left says 59 however the amount left is 58.						Sam Dowd
3/10/yr	4pm	Mouth	58	one	57	Sam Dowd
3/11/yr 7:06am Late entry for 3-10-yr 8am med was given and not subtracted at that time.						Jenna Sherman
3/11/yr	8am	Mouth	57	one	56	Jenna Sherman
3/11/yr	4pm	Mouth	56	one	55	Amanda Smith
3/12/yr	8am	Mouth	55	one	54	Jenna Sherman

2020 The Massachusetts Departments of Public Health, Developmental Services, Mental Health, Children and Families and the Rehabilitation Commission

Massachusetts | Responsibilities in Action   232

Requirement: Two Certified staff must verify a countable medication refill.

Scenario: A countable medication is delivered. You are the only Certified staff present.

Responsibility: You add the medication into the count when delivered. The second Certified staff verifies the amount delivered when they arrive to work.

2| P a g e

Name: David Cook

Doctor: Dr. Black

Pharmacy: Greenleaf

Medication and Strength: Phenobarbital 32.4mg

Directions: Take 3 tablets by mouth once daily in evening

___ Original Entry or

_X_ Transferred from page 1

Prescription Number: N671

Prescription Date: Feb. 17, yr

Date	Time	Route	Amount on Hand	Amount Used	Amount Left	Signature
3/3/yr	9am		Page Transfer		0	Amanda Smith / Jenna Sherman
3/3/yr	10am		Received from pharmacy		30	Sam Dowd / John Craig
3/3/yr	8pm	Mouth	30	Three	27	Jenna Sherman
3/4/yr	8pm	Mouth	27	Three	24	Amanda Smith
3/5/yr	8pm	Mouth	24	Three	21	Amanda Smith
3/6/yr	8pm	Mouth	21	Three	18	Amanda Smith
3/7/yr	8pm	Mouth	18	Three	15	Jenna Sherman
3/8/yr	8pm	Mouth	15	Three	12	Jenna Sherman
3/9/yr	9:45am	Received 60 tabs from pharmacy 72				John Craig
3/9/yr	2:30pm	Verifying 60 tabs received				Sam Dowd
3/9/yr	8pm	Mouth	72	Three	69	Jenna Sherman

Massachusetts | Responsibilities in Action

233

Requirement: Two Certified staff must verify a countable medication received from the pharmacy.

Scenario: You notice on a count sheet there is an increase in the 'amount left column' with no explanation.

Responsibility: You check the countable medication. You document what you find and notify the Supervisor.

The Supervisor will speak to the staff who added the medication into the count without an explanation.

5| P a g e

Name: Ellen Tracey   _X_ Original Entry or

Doctor: Dr. Glass   ____Transferred from page __

Pharmacy: Greenleaf   Prescription Number: N458

Medication and Strength: Lorazepam 0.5mg   Prescription Date: March 3, yr

Directions: Take 2 tablets by mouth twice daily and 1 tablet by mouth once daily PRN, anxiety. Give PRN dose at least 4 hours apart from scheduled dose. See Support Plan.

Date	Time	Route	Amount on Hand	Amount Used	Amount Left	Signature
3/3/yr	9am		Received from pharmacy		30	Linda White/Sam Dowd
3/3/yr	8pm	mouth	30	two	28	Amanda Smith
3/4/yr	8am	mouth	28	two	26	John Craig
3/4/yr	8pm	mouth	26	two	24	Sam Dowd
3/5/yr	8am	mouth	24	two	112	John Craig
3/5/yr	8pm	mouth	112	two	110	John Craig
3/6/yr 7:09am The amount left column increases from 24 to 112. See the 3-5-yr 8am entry. There is a second blister pack of ninety Lorazepam 0.5mg tabs that accounts for the increased number minus the dose that was administered after the medication was received. Linda White, Supervisor notified.						Jenna Sherman
3/6/yr	8am	mouth	110	two	108	Jenna Sherman

Massachusetts | Responsibilities in Action

Requirement: Discontinued (or expired) countable controlled medication must remain on count until disposed with a Supervisor present.

Scenario: A countable controlled medication is discontinued. You are working with another Certified staff but your Supervisor will not be present until the next day.

Responsibility: You mark the medication as discontinued on the medication sheet and write a progress note indicating the HCP discontinued the medication on the day it happened. When your Supervisor is available the medication is disposed. The reason for disposal is included as well as the corresponding 'Item#' on the disposal form. The amount left column is 'zeroed out' indicating the medication is no longer physically present to count. Your Supervisor will update the index to note the medication is no longer on count.

15| P a g e

Name: Scott Green

Doctor: Dr. S. Pratt

Pharmacy: Greenleaf

Medication and Strength: Zolpidem 5mg

____ Original Entry or

_X_ Transferred from page 9

Prescription Number: N558

Prescription Date: Apr. 2, yr

Directions: Take 1 tablet by mouth once daily PRN at bedtime per Scott's request for difficulty sleeping

Date	Time	Route	Amount on Hand	Amount Used	Amount Left	Signature
4/3/yr	9am	*Page Transfer*			30	*Linda White*/Sam Dowd
4/6/yr	9:38pm	mouth	30	One	29	Jenna Sherman
4-21-yr 2pm Scott told the HCP at today's appointment he is sleeping well. A year of sleep data and the number of times Scott requested Zolpidem was given to the HCP. The HCP wrote an order to discontinue Zolpidem. Linda White, Supervisor notified that med needs to be disposed. _____ Sam Dowd						
4/22/yr 9:17am twenty-nine Zolpidem tabs discontinued by Scott's HCP on 4/21/yr were disposed. See Item #37-yr.					*0*	*Linda White*/**Sam Dowd**

Requirement: Countable controlled medication that is dropped must be kept on count until disposed in the presence of two Certified staff.

Scenario: A countable controlled medication is dropped. You are working alone or with another staff who is not MAP Certified.

Responsibility: You write a progress note indicating the medication was dropped on the day it happened. When a second Certified staff and or your Supervisor is available the medication is disposed. The reason for disposal is included.

14| P a g e

Name: Tanisha Johnson
Doctor: Dr. Chen Lee
Pharmacy: Greenleaf
Medication and Strength: Phenobarbital 32.4mg
Directions: Take 2 tablets by mouth once daily in evening

____ Original Entry or
__X__ Transferred from page __4__
Prescription Number: N538
Prescription Date: Apr. 2, yr

Date	Time	Route	Amount on Hand	Amount Used	Amount Left	Signature
4/3/yr	9pm		*Page Transfer*		60	*John Craig*/Sam Dowd
4/3/yr	8pm	mouth	60	two	58	*Amanda Smith*
4/4/yr 7:43pm Med cup holding two tablets knocked off table and fell on floor. Placed in med cup and locked waiting for disposal. Linda White, Supervisor notified. _____ *Amanda Smith*						
4/4/yr	8pm	mouth	58	two	56	*Amanda Smith* *
4/5/yr 3:06pm The 8pm dose (two tabs) on 4/4/yr was dropped. The two tabs are now disposed. See Item #10-yr. 54						Sam Dowd/*John Craig*
4/5/yr	8pm	mouth	54	two	52	*Amanda Smith*

* The 4-4-yr 8pm entry indicates that after Amanda Smith documented the dropped medication, she then removed two additional tablets in preparation for the medication to be administered as scheduled.

Requirement: Documentation errors must be properly corrected.

Scenario: You enter incorrect documentation in the Count Book.

Responsibility: You correct the error. The original entry must remain legible.

20| P a g e

Name: Tanisha Johnson   _____ Original Entry or
Doctor: Dr. Chen Lee   _X_ Transferred from page 10
Pharmacy: Greenleaf   Prescription Number: N236
Medication and Strength: Clonazepam 1mg   Prescription Date: March 3, yr
Directions: Take 1 tablet by mouth twice daily at 8am and 4pm

Date	Time	Route	Amount on Hand	Amount Used	Amount Left	Signature
3/9/yr	9am		Page Transfer		60	John Craig/Sam Dowd
3/9/yr	4pm	Mouth	60	one	59	Amanda Smith
3/10/yr	8am	Mouth	59	One	58	Sam Dowd
3/10/yr	4pm	Mouth	58	One	57	Jenna Sherman
3/11/yr	8am	Mouth	57	One	56	Amanda Smith
3/11/yr	4pm	Mouth	56	One	55	Sam Dowd
3/12/yr	8am	Mouth	55	One	54	Jenna Sherman
3/12/yr	4pm	Mouth	54	One	~~54~~ error AS 53	Amanda Smith
3/13/yr	8am	Mouth	53	One	52	John Craig
3/13/yr	4pm	Mouth	52	One	51	Sam Dowd
~~3/13/yr~~	~~8am~~	~~Mouth~~	~~51~~	~~One~~	~~50~~	~~John Craig~~ error JC error JC
3/14/yr	8am	Mouth	51	One	50	John Craig

Massachusetts | Responsibilities in Action

Requirement: A HCP order must be copied as written when transcribing.

Scenario: The HCP orders a generic medication and the pharmacy supplies the generic medication ordered.

Responsibility: You will transcribe only the generic name of the medication. 'NA', which means 'not applicable', is written in the space next to the word 'brand'.

Month and Year: August, yr   MEDICATION ADMINISTRATION SHEET   Allergies: none

Start	Generic **Erythromycin**	Hour	1	2	3	4	5	6	7	8	9	10	11	12	13	14	15	16	17	18	19	20	21	22	23	24	25	26	27	28	29	30	31
8/3/yr	Brand **NA**	8am	X	X	X											X	X	X	X	X	X	X	X	X	X	X	X	X	X	X	X	X	X
	Strength **333mg** Dose **666mg**																																
Stop	Amount **2 tabs** Route **mouth**	4pm	X	X												X	X	X	X	X	X	X	X	X	X	X	X	X	X	X	X	X	X	X
8/13/yr	Frequency **Three times daily**	8pm	X	X												X	X	X	X	X	X	X	X	X	X	X	X	X	X	X	X	X	X	X

Special instructions: **for 10 days**   *Reason:* **Sinus infection**

Requirement: A HCP order must be copied as written when transcribing.

Scenario: The HCP orders a topical generic medication and the pharmacy supplies the topical generic medication ordered.

Responsibility: You will transcribe the topical generic medication. The percentage of a topical medication is part of the medication name. The dose, the strength and the amount are the specific amount (which may be compared to a coin size and or a 'pea' size, etc.) as written in the HCP order.

Month and Year: April, yr   MEDICATION ADMINISTRATION SHEET   Allergies: none

Start	Generic hydrocortisone cream 0.05%	Hour	1	2	3	4	5	6	7	8	9	10	11	12	13	14	15	16	17	18	19	20	21	22	23	24	25	26	27	28	29	30	31
4/1/yr	Brand NA																																
	Strength dime size Dose dime size																																
Stop	Amount dime size Route topical																																
cont	Frequency daily in the evening	8pm																															

Special instructions: apply to right elbow   *Reason:* dermatitis

Massachusetts | Responsibilities in Action   238

2020 The Massachusetts Departments of Public Health, Developmental Services, Mental Health, Children and Families and the Rehabilitation Commission

Requirement: When a medication occurrence happens or is discovered you must begin the 'Procedure following a Medication Occurrence' (see Unit 9).

Scenario: During blister pack monitoring you determine that a medication was not administered for a specific date and time although there are initials in the medication box. The medication is not documented as subtracted on the count sheet. The count is correct.

Responsibility: You begin the 'Procedure following a Medication Occurrence'. After the person is cared for and the procedure is followed, you write a medication progress note indicating the date and time it was discovered that the medication was not administered, who was notified and what you were instructed to do. You do not circle the initials. The staff who initialed will write a late entry medication progress note.

Month and Year: March, yr   MEDICATION ADMINISTRATION SHEET   Allergies: none

Start	Generic Clonazepam		Hour	1	2	3	4	5	6	7	8	9	10	11	12	13	14	15	16	17	18	19	20	21	22	23	24	25	26	27	28	29	30	31
8/31/yr	Brand Klonopin		8am	TM	TM	SD	SD	SD	SD	JC	JC	AW																						
	Strength 1mg Dose 1mg																																
Stop	Amount 1 tab Route mouth		4pm	JS	SD	AW	AW	AW	AW	JS	SD																							
Cont	Frequency twice daily 8am and 4pm																																

Special Instructions: *Reason: decrease seizures*

Name   Tanisha Johnson   **MEDICATION PROGRESS NOTE**

Date	Time	Medication	Dose	Given	Not Given	Refused	Other	Reason (for giving/not giving)	Results and/or Response	Staff Signature
3-9-yr 11:15am During routine blister pack monitoring it was noted there are no initials, date, time indicating that a Clonazepam tablet was removed for the 3-8-yr 8am dose. The medication box for Tanisha's 3-8-yr 8:00am dose of Clonazepam is initialed. I contacted Forrest Greenleaf, pharmacist, MAP Consultant. Mr. Greenleaf recommended continuing to administer medication as prescribed. Linda White, Supervisor										
3-11-yr 9:49am Late entry - the 3-8-yr 8am Clonazepam entry is initialed as administered, however, was not. ——————— John Craig										

See next page for the corresponding blister pack that was reviewed by the Supervisor.

Massachusetts | Responsibilities in Action   239

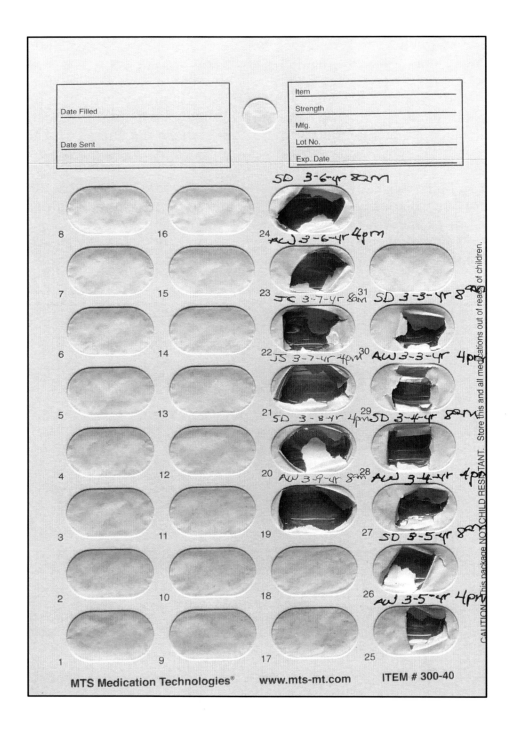

In addition, a medication occurrence report must be submitted to the MAP Coordinator within 7 days of the discovery.

Requirement: When a medication occurrence happens or is discovered you must begin the 'Procedure following a Medication Occurrence' (see Unit 9).

Scenario: You realize you administered medication to the wrong person. You begin the 'Procedure following a Medication Occurrence'. After checking to see if the person is okay, the MAP Consultant is contacted and recommends that the person be brought to the emergency room.

Responsibility: After the person is cared for, you complete all necessary documentation, including the count sheet page of the housemate's medication administered to the wrong person and the DPH medication occurrence report form.

6| P a g e

Name: Juanita Gomez

Doctor: Dr. Jones

Pharmacy: Greenleaf

Medication and Strength: Tramadol 50mg

Directions: Take 1 tablet by mouth twice daily

__X__ Original Entry or

_____ Transferred from page___

Prescription Number: N569

Prescription Date: March 2, yr

Date	Time	Route	Amount on Hand	Amount Used	Amount Left	Signature
3/3/yr	9am		Received from pharmacy		60	Linda White/Sam Dowd
3/3/yr	8pm	mouth	60	one	59	Amanda Smith
3/4/yr	8am	mouth	59	One	58	Sam Dowd
3/4/yr	8pm	mouth	58	One	57	Amanda Smith
3/5/yr	8am	mouth	57	One	56	John Craig
3/5/yr 8:43am One Tramadol 50mg tablet was removed and administered to housemate. ————————					55	John Craig

2020 The Massachusetts Departments of Public Health, Developmental Services, Mental Health, Children and Families and the Rehabilitation Commission

Department of Public Health Medication Administration Program
MEDICATION OCCURRENCE REPORT (side one)

Agency Name	Amercare	Date of Discovery	3-5-yr
Individual's Name	Tanisha Johnson	Time of Discovery	8:51am
Site Address (street)	45 Shade Street	Date(s) of Occurrence	3-5-yr
City/Town Zip Code	Treetop MA 00000	Time(s) of Occurrence	8:43am
Site Telephone No.	000-000-0000	DPH Registration No.	MAP 00001

A) Type Of Occurrence (As per regulation, contact MAP Consultant)

- 1 **X** Wrong Individual
- 2 ☐ Wrong Dose
- 3 ☐ Wrong Route
- 4 ☐ Wrong Medication (includes medication given without an order)
- 5 ☐ Wrong Time (includes medication not given in appropriate timeframe)
- ☐ Omission (subgroup of 'wrong time'--medication not given or forgotten)

B) Medication(s) Involved

	Medication Name	Dosage	Frequency/Time	Route
As Ordered:	not ordered for this Individual			
As Given:	Tramadol	50mg	8:43am	mouth
As Ordered:	not ordered for this individual			
As Given:	Phenytoin	200mg	8:43am	mouth
As Ordered:	not ordered for this individual			
As Given:	Docusate liquid	200mg	8:43am	mouth

C) MAP Consultant Contacted (Check all that apply)

Type	Name	Date Contacted	Time Contacted
☐ Registered Nurse			
☐ Registered Pharmacist			
X Health Care Provider	Dr. Chen Lee	3-5-yr	8:53am

D) Hotline Events

of the events below follow the occurrence? X Yes ☐ No

If yes, check all that apply below, and within 24 hours of discovery fax this form to DPH (617) 753-8046 or call to notify DPH at (617) 983-6782 and notify your DMH/DCF or DDS MAP Coordinator.
For All Occurrences, forward reports to your DMH/DCF or DDS MAP Coordinator within 7 days.

X Medical Intervention (see Section E below)	☐ Illness	☐ Injury	☐ Death

E) MAP Consultant's Recommended Action

Medical Intervention X Yes ☐ No   If Yes, Check all that apply.

☐ Health Care Provider Visit	☐ Lab Work or Other Tests	☐ Clinic Visit
X Emergency Room Visit	☐ Hospitalization	

☐ Other: Please describe

F) Supervisory Review/Follow-up

Contributing Factors: Check all that apply.

- 1 ☐ Failure to Properly Document Administration
- 2 ☐ Medication not Available (Explain Below)
- 3a ☐ Medication Administered by Non-Certified Staff (includes instances of expired or revoked Certification)
- 3b ☐ Medication Administered by a licensed nurse, employed on site. LPN ☐ RN ☐
- 3c ☐ Medication Administered by a licensed nurse, not employed on site (e.g., VNA)
- 4 ☐ Improperly Labeled by Pharmacy
- 5 ☐ Failure to Accurately Record and/or Transcribe an Order
- 6 ☐ Failure to Accurately Take or Receive a Telephone Order
- 7 ☐ Medication Had Been Discontinued
- 8 **X** Other (Narrative Required)

Narrative: (If additional space is required, continue in box F-1) Staff answered the telephone while preparing medications. Staff then administered a housemates' medication to Tanisha. Tanisha's 8am medication had been administered earlier as prescribed; Luminal 64.8mg by mouth and Klonopin 1mg by mouth. Tanisha was observed in the emergency room for 4 hours and then was released with no new HCP orders. Retraining planned for the involved staff and all other staff will include topic of mindfulness during medication administration and having someone else answer telephone.

Print Name	Print Title	Date
Linda White	Supervisor	3-5-yr
Contact phone	**E-mail**	
121-121-1212	lw@aol.net	

2020 The Massachusetts Departments of Public Health, Developmental Services, Mental Health, Children and Families and the Rehabilitation Commission

Massachusetts | Responsibilities in Action

Requirement: When a medication occurrence happens or is discovered you must begin the 'Procedure following a Medication Occurrence' (see Unit 9).

Scenario: The medication system in your work location is under review by your Supervisor and you are assisting. Your Supervisor asks you about a recently obtained HCP order for a cough medication for Juanita, who was just admitted from the emergency room to the hospital for a cough that worsened.

The order was for dextromethorphan hydrobromide liquid 30 mg by mouth every 8 hours for 7 days. The pharmacy label strength was printed as 15mg per 15mL. The directions were to give 30mL. You explain to your Supervisor that to measure, all staff used household spoons. This was the first liquid medication ever ordered in this home. There are no liquid measuring devices on site as paper medication cups are used for tablets. Juanita had 3 doses administered before the hospitalization.

Responsibility: Your Supervisor begins the 'Procedure following a Medication Occurrence' after identifying the 3 wrong doses and completes all necessary documentation including the DPH medication occurrence report form. All staff will be trained regarding using an appropriate measuring device (see Unit 7).

Massachusetts | Responsibilities in Action

Department of Public Health Medication Administration Program
MEDICATION OCCURRENCE REPORT (side one)

Agency Name	Amercare	Date of Discovery	5-14-yr
Individual's Name	Juanita Gomez	Time of Discovery	9:11am
Site Address (street)	45 Shade Street	Date(s) of Occurrence	5-13-yr to 5-14-yr
City/Town Zip Code	Treetop MA 00000	Time(s) of Occurrence	5-13-yr 3pm-11pm 5-14-yr 7am
Site Telephone No.	000-000-0000	DPH Registration No.	MAP 00001

(Right margin, rotated text: 2020 The Massachusetts Departments of Public Health, Developmental Services, Mental Health, Children and Families and the Rehabilitation Commission)

A)   Type Of Occurrence (As per regulation, contact MAP Consultant)

1	☐	Wrong Individual	4	☐	Wrong Medication (includes medication given without an order)
2	X	Wrong Dose	5	☐	Wrong Time (includes medication not given in appropriate timeframe)
3	☐	Wrong Route		☐	Omission (subgroup of 'wrong time'--medication not given or forgotten)

B)   Medication(s) Involved

	Medication Name	Dosage	Frequency/Time	Route
As Ordered:	dextromethorphan hydrobromide liquid	30 mg (30mL)	every 8 hours for 7 days	mouth
As Given:	dextromethorphan hydrobromide liquid	unknown	5-13-yr 3pm, 11pm 5-14-yr 7am	mouth
As Ordered:				
As Given:				
As Ordered:				
As Given:				

C)   MAP Consultant Contacted (Check all that apply)

Type	Name	Date Contacted	Time Contacted
☐ Registered Nurse			
☐ Registered Pharmacist			
X Health Care Provider	Dr. Richard Black	5-14-yr	9:47am

D)   Hotline Events

of the events below follow the occurrence? X Yes ☐ No

If yes, check all that apply below, and within 24 hours of discovery fax this form to DPH (617) 753-8046 or call to notify DPH at (617) 983-6782 and notify your DMH/DCF or DDS MAP Coordinator.
For All Occurrences, forward reports to your DMH/DCF or DDS MAP Coordinator within 7 days.

X Medical Intervention (see Section E below)	X Illness	☐ Injury	☐ Death

E)   MAP Consultant's Recommended Action

Medical Intervention   X Yes ☐ No   If Yes, Check all that apply.

☐ Health Care Provider Visit	X Lab Work or Other Tests	☐ Clinic Visit
X Emergency Room Visit	X Hospitalization	

X Other: Please describe Chest x-ray

F)   Supervisory Review/Follow-up

Contributing Factors: Check all that apply.

1	☐	Failure to Properly Document Administration	4	☐	Improperly Labeled by Pharmacy
2	☐	Medication not Available (Explain Below)	5	☐	Failure to Accurately Record and/or Transcribe an Order
3a	☐	Medication Administered by Non-Certified Staff (includes instances of expired or revoked Certification)	6	☐	Failure to Accurately Take or Receive a Telephone Order
3b	☐	Medication Administered by a licensed nurse, employed on site. LPN ☐ RN ☐	7	☐	Medication Had Been Discontinued
3c	☐	Medication Administered by a licensed nurse, not employed on site (e.g., VNA)	8	X	Other (Narrative Required)

Narrative: (If additional space is required, continue in box F-1) All staff involved used household spoons. Paper medication cups are used for tablets. Juanita's cough worsened after 3 doses of cough medication and she had difficulty breathing. The HCP was contacted and an ER visit followed. Lab work and a chest x-ray were completed. She was admitted to the hospital diagnosed with pneumonia. Retraining is planned for all staff regarding the use of an appropriate liquid measuring device.

Print Name	Print Title	Date
Linda White	Supervisor	5-14-yr
Contact phone	**E-mail**	
121-121-1212	lw@aol.net	

Massachusetts | Responsibilities in Action   244

Words You Should Know

Abbreviation - A shortened form of a word or phrase.

Accuracy check - A review of the new month's medication sheets completed by two Certified and/or licensed staff, ensuring that all information on the medication sheet is complete and correct.

Adverse Response - A severe side effect.

Allergic Reaction - When the body's immune system reacts to a medication as if it were a foreign substance.

Amount - The number of tablets, capsules or mL needed to equal the dose ordered by the HCP.

Anaphylactic Reaction - A severe, dangerous, life threatening allergic reaction which requires immediate medical attention, such as calling 911.

Authorized Prescriber - Health Care Provider (HCP; see HCP below).

Blister Pack Monitoring - A medication tracking mechanism. Documentation by staff, on the back of the blister pack, each time a tablet or capsule is removed from the package.

Brand name medication - A medication created and named by the specific pharmaceutical company that created it.

Chain of Custody - an unbroken documentation trail of accountability of the physical security of the medications.

Communication - Exchanging of information; this can be accomplished verbally, in writing and/or in the form of listening, body language, tone of voice.

Confidentiality - Keeping information about the people you support private; information to be shared on a 'need to know' basis.

Controlled Medication - Schedule VI medication which requires a prescription to obtain it from the pharmacy; must be single locked and is not required to be tracked in the Count Book.

Countable Controlled Medication - Schedule II-V medication, which requires a prescription to obtain it from the pharmacy; must be double locked and tracked in a Count Book.

Massachusetts | Responsibilities in Action

Countable Controlled Substance Book - A book used to document and track schedule II-V medications.

Count Book - Another name for the Countable Controlled Substance Book. A book used to track all countable controlled (schedule II-V) medication in a program.

Count Sheet - The middle section of the Count Book used to track the amount of each countable medication when added or subtracted.

Count Signature Sheets - The last section of the Count Book used by staff to document when responsibility for the countable medications is transferred from one staff to another staff.

DCF - Department of Children and Families.

DDS - Department of Developmental Services.

Desired Effect - When a medication does exactly what it was intended to do; the person experiences the beneficial results of the medication.

Dietary Supplements - Products not regulated by the federal government that contain a dietary ingredient such as vitamins, minerals, herbs or other substances.

Discontinue - When the HCP orders a medication or treatment to be stopped; typically abbreviated as D/C or DC.

Disposal - To render a medication unusable and dispose; must be documented on a Disposal Record.

Disposal Record - Document used to track the disposal of all prescription medication.

DMH - Department of Mental Health.

Documentation - To prove something by writing it down; your writing of what happened should tell a story from beginning to end.

Dose - How much medication the HCP orders the person to receive each time the medication is to be administered.

DPH - Department of Public Health.

Emergency Contact List - A single list of contact names and telephone numbers clearly posted for quick and easy staff reference including: MAP Consultants, Poison Control and other emergency numbers (911, fire, police).

Everyday Reporting - Exchanging information on routine, day to day matters.

Massachusetts | Responsibilities in Action

Expiration Date - Last date a medication may be administered.

Fax Health Care Provider Order - A signed and dated HCP order that is obtained via a fax machine. A fax order is a legal order.

Frequency - Also referred to as 'time'; how often the medication is ordered to be administered.

Generic name medication - A medication known by its chemical name. Many different pharmaceutical companies often manufacture generic named medications.

HCP Encounter/Consult/Order Form - Different names used for the same form; the form used by the HCP to write orders.

Health Care Provider (HCP) - A person who is registered in the state of Massachusetts to prescribe medication.

Health Care Provider Order - A set of detailed orders/instructions many times medication related, however, sometimes not related to medication, written by the HCP for each person.

High Alert Medication - A medication requiring additional training and competencies before certified staff can administer the medication.

Hotline Medication Occurrence - When one of the 5 rights goes wrong during the medication administration process; followed by medical intervention, illness, injury or death.

Immediate Reporting - Exchanging information right away.

Index - The first section of the Count Book. The index lists the person's name, medication name and strength and count sheet page number for each countable medication.

Leave of Absence (LOA) - Code used on a medication sheet when medication is released from a person's home to a family member or a responsible friend to administer who is not required to be MAP Certified or a licensed staff.

Leave of Absence Form - Document used to track medication when sent on a LOA.

Lot Number - A number assigned to each 'batch' of medication produced.

MAP - Medication Administration Program.

Massachusetts | Responsibilities in Action 247

MAP Consultant - A licensed professional who is available 24/7 to answer your medication questions. A MAP Consultant is a registered nurse (RN), registered pharmacist or HCP.

MAP Policy Manual - Single, topically organized source of MAP information and policies.

MCSR - Massachusetts Controlled Substances Registration.

Medication - A substance that when put into or onto the body will change one or more ways the body works.

Medication Administration Process - When administering medication, what you must do to prepare, administer and complete each time you give a medication.

Medication Grid - The right side of a medication sheet used to document your initials after administering a medication.

Medication Information - A resource that gives information about a medication.

Medication Information Sheet - A resource for medication information typically obtained from the pharmacy.

Medication Interaction - A mixing of medications in the body that will either increase or decrease the effects and/or side effects of one or both of the medications. In addition to medications interacting with each other, medications can also interact with dietary supplements, other substances (alcohol, nicotine and caffeine) and certain foods.

Medication Occurrence - When one of the 5 rights goes wrong during medication administration.

Medication Occurrence Report (MOR) - Document used to track and report each time one of the 5 rights goes wrong during medication administration.

Medication Ordering and Receiving Log - Documentation of when a program orders medication and when received from the pharmacy.

Medication Outcome - The result a medication produces after it is administered; Desired Effect, No Effect Noted and/or Side Effects.

Medication Release Document - Document used to track medication when moved from one location to another location.

Medication Reconciliation - Comparing the hospital discharge orders to the orders the person had prior to admission; discrepancies are clarified with the prescribing HCP.

Massachusetts | Responsibilities in Action

Medication Record - A medication tracking record which typically contains an Emergency Fact Sheet, HCP orders, medication sheets and medication information sheets for each person living at the program.

Medication Refill - A number on the pharmacy label indicating how many times the medication may be obtained from the pharmacy.

Medication Refusal - When a person will not take the medication from you either by: saying 'No", spitting the medication right back out, spitting the medication out later or intentionally vomiting within one half hour of taking it.

Medication Schedule - A number (schedule) assigned by the Drug Enforcement Agency (DEA) to a prescription medication based on the medication's potential to be abused; the lower the number the more likely the medication is to be abused.

Medication Sensitivity - How each person responds to the same medication. Factors that affect medication sensitivity include: age, weight, gender, general health, medical history, level of physical activity and the use of other medication(s) or dietary supplements.

Medication Sheet - Document used to track the administration of each person's medication on a monthly basis.

Microgram (mcg) - one millionth of a gram.

Mindfulness - Always paying attention to what you are doing; focusing on the task at hand.

MRC - Massachusetts Rehabilitation Commission.

No Effect Noted - A medication outcome when a medication is taken for a specific reason and the symptoms continue; no effects are noted from the medication.

Nutritional Supplements - Conventional food items such as Ensure, gastric tube feedings or Carnation Instant Breakfast; nutritional supplements are not medications and do not fall under MAP.

Objective Information - Factual information that you can see, hear, smell, feel and/or measure.

Observation - The process of watching someone carefully in order to obtain information.

Omission - Subcategory of wrong time; occurs when the medication is not administered.

Massachusetts | Responsibilities in Action

Oral - A route; when a medication is taken by mouth.

ODT - orally dissolving tablet. A tablet designed to be dissolved on the tongue rather than swallowed whole.

Over-the-Counter (OTC) Medication - Medications that may be purchased without a prescription.

Paradoxical Reaction - A response to a medication that is the opposite of what the medication was intended to produce.

Parameters - A set of rules or guidelines that tell you how or when a medication should or should not be administered.

Pharmacy manifest - Documentation provided by the pharmacy listing the names and amounts of medications received by the program. This form often contains more than one person's medications.

Pharmacy Receipt - A document received from the pharmacy listing how many tablets, capsules or mL of each medication was dispensed to the program.

Post - Documentation completed by staff on the HCP order (under the HCP signature) after a medication is transcribed.

Prescription - A set of instructions from the HCP to the pharmacist telling the pharmacist what medication to prepare and how to give it for the person it is prescribed. The pharmacist uses the prescription to print a pharmacy label.

Prescription number - A number on the pharmacy label used to obtain refills; often referred to as the 'Rx' number.

Principles of Medication Administration - Foundation of the Medication Administration Process including Mindfulness, Supporting Abilities and Communication.

Prior Authorization - Approval from an insurance company, required prior to the pharmacy being able to fill a prescription; to ensure the medication will be paid for.

PRN - Latin term meaning a medication to be given only when needed.

PRN medication - Medication that is ordered to be administered only when needed for a specific health issue.

Protocol - A detailed HCP order that includes instructions on when, how and why to give a medication. Typically used when the medication is ordered to help lessen physical symptoms such as seizures or constipation.

Massachusetts | Responsibilities in Action

Reporting - To give spoken or written information of something observed or told.

Route - The way in which the medication enters the body.

Rx - Abbreviation for a prescription number, used to obtain refills.

Shoulder to Shoulder Count - A specific procedure which transfers responsibility for the safety and security of the medications, from one staff to another staff. Conducted by 2 Certified staff each time the medication storage keys change hands.

Shoulder to Shoulder Disposal - A specific procedure conducted by 2 Certified staff which renders a medication useless.

Side Effect - Result from a medication that is not wanted or intended even if the desired effect is achieved. Side effects can range from mild to severe.

Single Person Count - Procedure conducted when there is only one Certified and/or licensed staff available to count the countable medication; typically completed when only one staff is on duty when putting the medication storage keys into or taking them out of the coded lock box.

Special Instructions - Information listed on the HCP order and/or pharmacy label giving additional information about medication administration.

Start Date - The date a person is scheduled to receive the first dose of a medication.

Stop Date - The date a person is scheduled to receive the last dose of a medication or if given continuously.

Strength - How much medication is contained within each tablet, capsule or mL.

Subjective Information - When a person speaks or signs and they tell you something.

Support Plan - A detailed HCP order that includes instructions on when, how and why to give a medication. Typically used when the medication is ordered to help lessen a behavior.

Supporting Abilities - Helping a person to be as independent as possible.

Tamper Resistant Packaging - A way the pharmacy packages a medication to physically limit how the medication is accessed.

Telephone Health Care Provider Order - Documentation of a HCP order taken by Certified staff while speaking with the HCP on the telephone. A telephone order must be signed by the HCP within 72 hours.

Toxicity - When a medication builds up in the body to the point where the body cannot handle it anymore; this can be life threating.

Transcribe - To copy information from one document and record it onto another document.

Transcription - The completed document after information has been recorded from one or more documents onto it.

Verify - Documentation completed by a second staff on the HCP order (under the HCP signature) after reviewing the first staff's completed transcription for accuracy.

Wrong Dose - When either too much or too little of a medication is administered at the scheduled time.

Wrong Medication - When medication is administered without a HCP order; includes using an expired or discontinued HCP order, administering past the stop date of a time limited medication order or administering one medication instead of another.

Wrong Person - When medication is administered to a person it is not ordered for either by misidentification, distraction or the medication was left unattended/not secured and someone else ingested it.

Wrong Route - When the medication is administered by a way (route) not ordered by the HCP.

Wrong Time - When the medication is administered too early, too late or parameters or instructions for use of the medication are not followed.

Answer Key

Unit 1

Page 17

1. F
2. F
3. T
4. F
5. T
6. F
7. T

Page 19

1. Juanita is able to nod her head 'yes' and ''no' to respond to a question or she may 'make a face' to show if she liked (smiled) or did not like (frowned) a flavor when tasting the pudding
   Related principle-communication
2. Allow Ellen to fill her own glass of water for medication administration
   Related principle- supporting abilities
3. Often switch the order of who you administer the medications to
   Related principle-mindfulness

Page 21

1. Anxiety defined as biting hands for more than 4 minutes and head slapping for longer than 30 seconds or more than 5 times in 4 minutes
2. No
3. Notify HCP

Unit 2

Page 24

1. O
2. O
3. S
4. O
5. S

Page 28

4. _√_ David states he has, 'sharp pain' when he bends his right knee. He frowns getting off the van and is limping. His right knee is now red, warm to touch and swollen. He has received Ibuprofen 400mg for right knee pain and his symptoms continue.

Unit 3

Page 33

Lisinopril   Omeprazole   Ibuprofen

Page 41

This product is a(n)
1. (b.) OTC Medication
2. Is a HCP order required for administration?   Yes
3. Is a pharmacy label required for administration? Yes
4. Is the product transcribed onto a medication sheet? Yes

This product is a(n)
1. (a.) Dietary Supplement
2. Is a HCP order required for administration?   Yes
3. Is a pharmacy label required for administration? Yes
4. Is the product transcribed onto a medication sheet? Yes

Massachusetts | Responsibilities in Action

Page 44

Sample Medication Information Sheet

Interactions: Tell your HCP of all the medications you are taking. Do not use with St. John's Wort. Using tramadol together with alcohol may increase side effects such as dizziness, drowsiness, confusion, and difficulty concentrating.

Page 46

1. B
2. C
3. G
4. L
5. K
6. E
7. F
8. J
9. H
10. I
11. A
12. D

Unit 4

Page 53

1. Dr. Black
2. Burning in throat after eating
3. Sam Dowd
4. No known allergies
5. Gastroesophageal reflux disease
6. Prilosec
7. Remain upright 30 minutes after eating

Page 54

HEALTH CARE PROVIDER ORDER

Name: Tanisha Johnson	Date: Feb. 2, yr
Health Care Provider: Dr. Chen Lee	Allergies: No known medication allergies
Reason for Visit: Complaining of soreness in back of mouth.	
Current Medications: √ Phenobarbital 64.8mg once daily in the evening by mouth √ Clonazepam 1mg twice daily at 8am and 4pm by mouth	
Staff Signature: *Sam Dowd*	Date: Feb. 2, yr
Health Care Provider Findings: Inflammation of gum-line on left side of mouth	
Medication/Treatment Orders: Amoxil Suspension 500mg every 12 hours for seven days by mouth	
Instructions: Notify HCP if Tanisha continues to complain of mouth soreness after 72 hours.	
Follow-up visit: Feb. 16, yr	Lab work or Tests: None
Signature: *Dr. Chen Lee*	Date: Feb. 2, yr

1. Circle the new medication order-see above
2. 500mg
3. Every 12 hours for seven days
4. Place a checkmark next to Tanisha's current medications-see above
5. No

Page 59

1. Yes

2. Record the order word-for-word on a HCP Order form. Read back the information given to you by the HCP to confirm you recorded it accurately. If you have trouble understanding the HCP, ask another staff to listen in as you take the order, then have staff read it back and sign the order too. If you do not know how to spell a spoken word, ask the HCP to spell it. Draw lines through any blank spaces in the order.

3. 72 hours

4. Yes

Page 62

3 tablets

Unit 5

Page 70

1 Rx # C201	**2** Greenleaf Pharmacy 20 Main Street Treetop, MA 00000	**3** 111-222-3434 **5** 3/4/yr

4 David Cook
6a Tramadol **7** 50mg
6b IC Ultram   Qty. 21 **8**

Take **9** 1 tablet **10** by mouth **11** every 8 hours for 7 days

12 Take with water

13 Dr. Black

14 Lot # 776-5433   **15** ED: 3/4/yr   **16** Refills: 0

Page 71

1. C
2. C
3. D
4. All

Page 72

1. You could give an incorrect dose of four 100mg tablets
2. It is a different color

Page 74

1. 120
2. 32
3. 28
4. no
5. a day too early
6. 28
7. to ensure medication is available to administer as ordered

Unit 6

Page 81

1.   T
2.   F
3.   T
4.   F
5.   T

Page 89

Write the number on the medication sheet of the term (p. 87) that corresponds with information to be transcribed, listed as numbers 1-14.

Month and Year: month, yr **1**   MEDICATION ADMINISTRATION SHEET   Allergies: **3**

Start **11**	Generic **4**		Hour 1 2 3 4 5 6 7 8 9 10 11 12 13 14 15 16 17 18 19 20 21 22 23 24 25 26 27 28 29 30 31
	Brand **5**		
	Strength **7**	Dose **6**	
Stop **12**	Amount **8**	Route **10**	
	Frequency **9**		

Special instructions: **13**   *Reason:* **14**

Start	Generic		Hour 1 2 3 4 5 6 7 8 9 10 11 12 13 14 15 16 17 18 19 20 21 22 23 24 25 26 27 28 29 30 31
	Brand		
	Strength	Dose	
Stop	Amount	Route	
	Frequency		

Special instructions: *Reason:*

Start	Generic		Hour 1 2 3 4 5 6 7 8 9 10 11 12 13 14 15 16 17 18 19 20 21 22 23 24 25 26 27 28 29 30 31
	Brand		
	Strength	Dose	
Stop	Amount	Route	
	Frequency		

Special instructions: *Reason:*

Start	Generic		Hour 1 2 3 4 5 6 7 8 9 10 11 12 13 14 15 16 17 18 19 20 21 22 23 24 25 26 27 28 29 30 31
	Brand		
	Strength	Dose	
Stop	Amount	Route	
	Frequency		

Special instructions: *Reason:*

Name: **2**	CODES		Signature		Signature
	DP-day program/day hab				
	LOA-leave of absence				
	P-packaged				
Site:	W-work				
	H-hospital, nursing home, rehab center				
	S-school				

Accuracy Check 1_____ Date_____ Time_____   Accuracy Check 2 _____ Date_____ Time_____

Massachusetts | Responsibilities in Action

Page 92

1.

Hour
10pm

2.

Hour
7:30am

Page 93

1.

Hour
4pm

2.

Hour
8am
8pm

1.

Hour
P
R
N

Massachusetts | Responsibilities in Action

Page 94

1. E
2. G
3. F
4. C
5. D
6. H
7. B
8. A

Page 102-103

1. 3/3/yr at 4pm
2. 3/3/yr
3. 3/13/yr at 8am
4. 3/13/yr
5. 3 times daily for 10 days
6. 8am, 4pm, 8pm
7. 666mg
8. 2 tabs
9. 333mg
10. Sam Dowd

Page 107

HEALTH CARE PROVIDER ORDER

Name: Tanisha Johnson	**Date:** Feb. 5, yr
Health Care Provider: Dr. Chen Lee	**Allergies:** No known medication allergies
Reason for Visit: Continues to complain of soreness in back of mouth	
Current Medications: Phenobarbital 64.8mg once daily at 8pm by mouth Clonazepam 1mg twice daily by mouth Amoxil Suspension 500mg every 12 hours for seven days by mouth	
Staff Signature: Sam Dowd	**Date:** Feb. 5, yr
Health Care Provider Findings: Increased inflammation of gum-line on left side of mouth	
Medication/Treatment Orders: DC Amoxil Suspension Cleocin HCL 300mg three times a day for 10 days by mouth	
Instructions: Notify HCP if Tanisha continues to complain of mouth soreness after 72 hours.	
Follow-up visit: February 16, yr	**Lab work or Tests:** None
Signature: Dr. Chen Lee	**Date:** Feb. 5, yr

Posted by: *Full Signature*   Date: *2/5/yr*   Time: *1pm*   Verified by: Date: Time:

Massachusetts | Responsibilities in Action

2020 The Massachusetts Departments of Public Health, Developmental Services, Mental Health, Children and Families and the Rehabilitation Commission

Page 108

Month and Year: February, yr   **MEDICATION ADMINISTRATION SHEET**   **Allergies: none**

Start	Generic Phenobarbital	Hour	1	2	3	4	5	6	7	8	9	10	11	12	13	14	15	16	17	18	19	20	21	22	23	24	25	26	27	28	29	30	31
8/31/yr	Brand Luminal																																	
	Strength 32.4mg Dose 64.8mg																																	
Stop	Amount 2 tabs Route mouth																																	
Cont.	Frequency Once daily at 8pm	8pm	TM	TM	TM	JS																												

Special instructions: Reason: seizures

Start	Generic Clonazepam	Hour	1	2	3	4	5	6	7	8	9	10	11	12	13	14	15	16	17	18	19	20	21	22	23	24	25	26	27	28	29	30	31
8/31/yr	Brand Klonopin	8am	KM	AS	KM	KM	AS																												
	Strength 1mg Dose 1mg																																	
Stop	Amount 1 tab Route mouth	4pm	TM	TM	TM	JS																												
Cont.	Frequency Twice daily 8am and 4pm																																	

Special instructions: Reason: seizures

Start	Generic Amoxicillin suspension	Hour	1	2	3	4	5	6	7	8	9	10	11	12	13	14	15	16	17	18	19	20	21	22	23	24	25	26	27	28	29	30	31
2/2/yr	Brand Amoxil suspension	8am	X	X	KM	KM	AS					X	X	X	X	X	X	X	X	X	X	X	X	X	X	X	X	X	X	X	X	X	X
	Strength 250mg/5mL Dose 500mg																																	
Stop	Amount 10mL Route																																	
2/9/yr	Frequency every 12 hours for 7 days	8pm	X	TM	TM	JS						X	X	X	X	X	X	X	X	X	X	X	X	X	X	X	X	X	X	X	X	X	X	X

D/C 2/5/yr initials   **D/C 2/5/yr initials**

Special instructions: Reason: gum inflammation

Start	Generic Clindamycin	Hour	1	2	3	4	5	6	7	8	9	10	11	12	13	14	15	16	17	18	19	20	21	22	23	24	25	26	27	28	29	30	31
2/5/yr	Brand Cleocin HCL	8am	X	X	X	X	X								X	X	X	X	X	X	X	X	X	X	X	X	X	X	X	X	X	X	X	X
	Strength 100mg Dose 300mg																																	
Stop	Amount 3 tabs Route mouth	4pm	X	X	X	X									X	X	X	X	X	X	X	X	X	X	X	X	X	X	X	X	X	X	X	X
2/15/yr	Frequency 3 times daily for 10 days	8pm	X	X	X	X									X	X	X	X	X	X	X	X	X	X	X	X	X	X	X	X	X	X	X	X

Special instructions: Take with 8 ounces of water   Reason: gum inflammation

	CODES		Signature		Signature
Name: Tanisha Johnson	**DP-day program/day hab**	KM	Kay Mathers	JC	John Craig
	LOA-leave of absence	AS	Amanda Smith		
Site: 45 Shade Street Treetop MA 00000	**P-packaged**	TM	Timothy Miller		
	W-work	SW	Serena Wilson		
	H-hospital, nursing home, rehab center	JS	Jenna Sherman		
	S-school	SD	Sam Dowd		

Accuracy Check 1 Sam Dowd   Date 1/31/yr   Time 9pm   Accuracy Check 2 John Craig   Date 1/31/yr   Time 9pm

Page 109

1. B
2. C
3. C
4. C
5. B

Unit 7

Page 112

Blood pressure

Page 114

Yes

Page 115

1. PRN medication
2. For complaints of right knee pain
3. No
4. 5PM
5. Notify HCP

Page 119

No. Aspirin EC is ordered. Aspirin was supplied.

Page 122

	Amount
1.	2 tablets
2.	2 tablets
3.	2 capsules
4.	3 tablets
5.	1 capsule
6.	4 tablets
7.	5 tablets
8.	2 capsules
9.	2 tablets
10.	2 tablets
11.	½ tablet

Page 125

4. _√_ Ask your Supervisor to arrange a specialized training for EpiPen® use

Page 130

1. HCP Order and pharmacy label
2. pharmacy label and medication sheet
3. pharmacy label and medication sheet

Match each check in the medication administration process to its corresponding reason.

Check 1   C

Check 2   A

Check 3   B

Massachusetts | Responsibilities in Action   265

2020 The Massachusetts Departments of Public Health, Developmental Services, Mental Health, Children and Families and the Rehabilitation Commission

Page 131

No. The frequency listed on the HCP order is 'daily in the evening' and the frequency listed on the pharmacy label is 'every evening at 8 PM' Note: if the HCP order is not time specific, the label should include the time of day ordered, not a specific time.

Page 133

1. T
2. T
3. F
4. T
5. F

Page 141

250mg

Page 142

1. 1200mg/15mL
   You should have filled to the 30mL line

Page 143

2. 100mg/5mL
   You should have filled to the 10mL line

Page 144

3. 262mg/15mL
   You should have filled to the 15mL line

Massachusetts | Responsibilities in Action

Page 149

Amount	
1.	20mL
2.	12mL
3.	4mL
4.	8mL
5.	10mL
6.	9mL
7.	8mL
8.	20mL
9.	15mL
10.	30mL
11.	20mL

Page 150

3. _√_ Call the pharmacy and request an appropriate measuring device.

Match the terms with the corresponding letter.

1. C

2. D

3. B

4. A

Page 150 continued

True (T) or False (F)

1. T
2. T
3. T
4. F
5. T
6. T

Pages 153-154

You should:

3. _√_ Ask David why he doesn't want to take the medication

David tells you he doesn't like the purple color of the tablet. You should:

4. _√_ Secure the medication, return in 15 minutes and offer it again

After 3 attempts, David still refuses the medication. You should first:

4. _√_ Notify Dr. Black of the refusal

Page 154

Using the medication sheet and corresponding progress note, document the medication refusal.

Your initials circled

Start	Generic **Omeprazole**		Hour	1	2	3	4	5	6	7	8	9	10	11	12	13	14	15	16	17	18	19	20	21	22	23	24	25	26	27	28	29	30	31
8/31/yr	Brand **Prilosec**																																
	Strength **20mg**	Dose **20mg**																															
Stop	Amount **1 tab**	Route **mouth**	4pm	WS	WD	JC ⃝																											
Cont.	Frequency **Once daily before supper**																																

Special instructions: Reason: **GERD**

MEDICATION PROGRESS NOTE   **March, yr**

3/4/yr 4:45pm David refused his 4pm dose of Prilosec. I attempted to administer it 3 times. Dr. Black and (your supervisor's name) notified.
_____Your full signature

Page 155

Class Discussion

1. So that the HCP will have enough information to make a decision about medication changes.
2. So that the HCP will be able to determine if the disruption in the administration of the medication may lead to the medication being less effective.
3. Scott could experience racing thoughts, which in his history may lead Scott to being a safety risk to himself and others in the community.

The most complete information to report to the prescribing HCP is:

Scott refused his antipsychotic medication on Friday and previously on Monday, Tuesday and Thursday.

Page 157

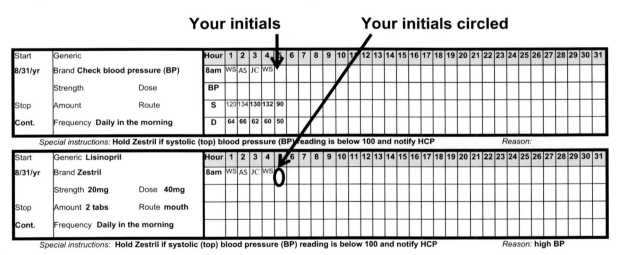

MEDICATION PROGRESS NOTE   March, yr

3/5/yr 8am Blood Pressure 90/50 Zestril 40mg held. (Name of HCP notified.) _____ Your full signature

Page 158

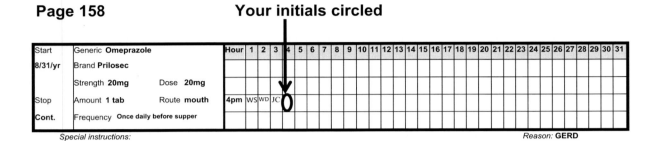

MEDICATION PROGRESS NOTE March, yr

3/4/yr 4PM Omeprazole 20mg held per HCP order to hold before scheduled test --- Your full signature

Page 160

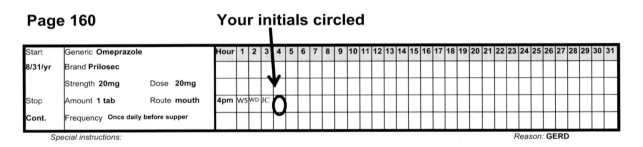

MEDICATION PROGRESS NOTE March, yr

3/4/yr 4PM Prilosec was unavailable. Spoke to Forrest Greenleaf at the Greenleaf Pharmacy. He stated medication will be delivered by 7:30pm. He stated to omit 4pm dose and give the next scheduled dose when due. (Name of your Supervisor) also notified _____ Your full signature

Unit 8

Page 164

Call the prescribing HCP to request a new prescription be submitted to the pharmacy.

Page 174

1. F
2. T
3. T
4. T
5. T

Page 175

3. _√_ Unlock the medication storage area, obtain the drug reference book for the Certified staff and relock.

Page 175

1. **N**
2. **N**
3. **N**

Page 175

1. The 'Chain of Custody' is broken and medications could be stolen.

2. To MAP Certified and/or licensed staff after conducting a two person count with them.

Page 176

Yes, (the tablets were popped out of order)

Page 181

Day Program Staff

1. V
2. OSA

Residential Program Staff

1. OSA
2. DP
3. LOA
4. V
5. W

Page 186 Class Discussion

Day program staff continued to give the discontinued medication. Residential staff should have faxed or sent a copy of the new order over to the day program.

Page 189

5 tablets

Page 205

1. two
2. Count Book
3. item number
4. Supervisor

Unit 9

Page 219

Number the 'Procedure Following a Medication Occurrence' in the order to be completed if you make or discover a medication occurrence

   7 Complete a Medication Occurrence Report

   4 Follow all recommendations given to you by the MAP Consultant

   5 Notify your supervisor

   2 Call 911, if needed

   6 Document what you did

   3 Call a MAP Consultant

   1 Check to see if the person is ok

Page 220

1. Wrong Person

2. Check to make sure the person is ok, if not call 911, if ok contact MAP consultant for recommendation

3. Medications should never be pre poured and never left unattended

4. Jim could have secured the medication before assisting with the emergency or taken the medication with him

Page 221

1. Wrong Medication

2. Check to see that Tanisha is ok, if not call 911, if ok contact MAP Consultant for recommendation

3. By looking at the HCP order (check #1 of the medication administration process)

Page 222

1. Wrong Dose

2. Check to see that Tanisha is ok, if not call 911, if ok contact MAP Consultant for recommendation

3. By looking at the pharmacy label to find the strength of the tablet and the amount to give to equal the dose

Page 224

1. Call the HCP for a refill

2. MAP Consultant

3. Omission

4. Refills should have been ordered at least one week before the medication ran out

Page 225

1. Wrong Route

2. Check to make sure Ellen is ok and if not call 911, if ok contact MAP Consultant for recommendation

3. Joe should have instructed the other staff to stop talking with him until he finished administering medications so he could have been mindful and completed his three checks before administering the medication

Massachusetts | Responsibilities in Action

Page 226

Match the term to the corresponding example

1.	C
2.	F
3.	A
4.	D
5.	B
6.	E

Ask Your Supervisor Specific to Your Work Location

1. Where is the MAP Massachusetts Controlled Substances Registration (MCSR) located?

2. Where is the MAP Policy manual located?

3. Where are MAP Consultants, poison control and other emergency numbers located?

4. Who is responsible for contacting the HCP to report changes observed in the people you support?

5. How is information shared between shifts, such as how new HCP orders are communicated if there is no staff present when you arrive for your shift?

6. Does anyone have HCP orders for 'high alert' medication?

7. Does anyone have HCP orders for 'high risk' for abuse Schedule VI medication and if so, how they are tracked?

8. How does the pharmacy identify countable controlled medication?

9. Where are the current (less than 2 years old) drug reference book and/or the current (less than 2 years old) medication information sheets located?

10. What HCP visit forms are required specific to the people you support?

11. Am I allowed to take a telephone order, if yes, where are the telephone order forms kept?

12. What method is used to obtain medication refills from the pharmacy?

13. What alternative pharmacy service is used to obtain medication if the typical pharmacy service is not available?

14. Are there HCP orders for antipsychotic medications requiring a Rogers Decision?

15. Where are medications requiring refrigeration stored?

16. How is the backup set of keys accessed, if needed?

17. What is the medication administration time schedule?

18. When will I receive training on all other routes medications are administered?

19. Is blister pack monitoring required?

20. Does the pharmacy supply automatic refills?   If yes, what system is used to cross check the medication I am expecting to receive to what the pharmacy delivers?

21. How are the new month's medication sheets generated and who is responsible for completing accuracy checks?

22. What is the communication system between the day program and the residential program?

23. What is the procedure regarding staff responsibilities when a person returns from a LOA?

24. Is the supervisor required for all medication disposals or may two Certified staff (no supervisor) dispose of a refused dose or a dropped dose of medication?

25. How are MORs submitted?

26. What is the policy/procedure regarding medication occurrence follow up?

Made in United States
North Haven, CT
17 July 2022